DATE DUE

AUG 1 1 2020			
GAYLORD			PRINTED IN U.S.A.

Great Careers

Food, Agriculture, and Natural Resources

with a High School Diploma

Titles in the *Great Careers* series

Great Careers

Food, Agriculture, and Natural Resources

with a High School Diploma

Amanda Kirk

Ferguson Publishing
An imprint of Infobase Publishing

Great Careers with a High School Diploma
Food, Agriculture, and Natural Resources

Copyright © 2008 by Infobase Publishing, Inc.

Ferguson
An imprint of Infobase Publishing
132 West 31st Street
New York, NY 10001

ISBN-13:978-0-8160-7046-6

Library of Congress Cataloging-in-Publication Data

Great careers with a high school diploma. — 1st ed.
    v. cm.
  Includes bibliographical references and index
  Contents: [1] Food, agriculture, and natural resources — [2] Construction and trades — [3] Communications, the arts, and computers — [4] Sales, marketing, business, and finance — [5] Personal care services, fitness, and education — [6] Health care, medicine, and science — [7] Hospitality, human services, and tourism — [8] Public safety, law, and security — [9] Manufacturing and transportation — [10] Armed forces.
  ISBN-13: 978-0-8160-7046-6 (v.1)
  ISBN-10: 0-8160-7046-6 (v.1)
  ISBN-13: 978-0-8160-7043-5 (v.2)
  ISBN-10: 0-8160-7043-1 (v.2)
[etc.]
1. Vocational guidance — United Sates. 2. Occupations — United Sates. 3. High school graduates — Employment — United Sates.
  HF5382.5.U5G677 2007
  331.702'330973 — dc22
                                                    2007029883

Produced by Print Matters, Inc.
Text design by A Good Thing, Inc.
Cover design by Salvatore Luongo

Printed in the United States of America

Sheridan PMI 10 9 8 7 6 5 4 3 2 1

This book is printed on acid-free paper.

Contents

How to Use This Book

This book, part of the Great Careers with a High School Diploma series, highlights in-demand careers that require no more than a high school diploma or the general educational development (GED) credential and offer opportunities for personal growth and professional advancement to motivated readers who are looking for a field that's right for them. The focus throughout is on the fastest-growing jobs with the best potential for advancement in the field. Readers learn about future prospects while discovering jobs they may never have heard of.

Knowledge—of yourself and about a potential career—is a powerful tool in launching yourself professionally. This book tells you how to use it to your advantage, explore job opportunities, and identify a good fit for yourself in the working world.

Each chapter provides the essential information needed to find not just a job but a career that draws on your particular skills and interests. All chapters include the following features:

- ⭐ "Is This Job for You?" presents a set of questions for you to answer about yourself to help you learn if you have what it takes to work in a given career.
- ⭐ "Let's Talk Money" and "Lets Talk Trends" provide at a glance crucial information about salary ranges and employment prospects.
- ⭐ "What You'll Do" provides descriptions of the essentials of each job.
- ⭐ "Where You'll Work" relates the details of the settings and the rules and patterns typical of that field.
- ⭐ "Your Typical Day" provides details about what a day on the job involves for each occupation.
- ⭐ "The Inside Scoop" presents firsthand information from someone working in the field.
- ⭐ "What You Can Do Now" provides advice on getting prepared for your future career.
- ⭐ "What Training You'll Need" discusses state requirements, certifications, and courses or other training you may need as you get started on your new career path.
- ⭐ "How to Talk Like a Pro" defines a few key terms that give a feel for the occupation.

- ⚡ "How to Find a Job" gives the practical how-tos of landing a position.
- ⚡ "Secrets for Success" and "Reality Check" share inside information on getting ahead.
- ⚡ "Some Other Jobs to Think About" lists similar related careers to consider.
- ⚡ "How You Can Move Up" outlines how people in each occupation turn a job into a career, advancing in responsibility and earnings power.
- ⚡ "Web Sites to Surf" lists Web addresses of trade organizations and other resources providing more information about the career.

In addition to a handy comprehensive index, the back of the book features an appendix providing invaluable information on job hunting strategies and techniques. This section provides general tips on interviewing, constructing a strong résumé, and gathering professional references. Use this book to discover a career that seems right for you—the tools to get you where you want to be are at your fingertips.

Introduction

For millions of Americans, life after high school means stepping into the real world. Each year more than 900,000 of the nation's 2.8 million high school graduates go directly into the workforce. Clearly, college isn't for everyone. Many people learn best by using their hands rather than by sitting in a classroom. Others find that the escalating cost of college puts it beyond reach, at least for the time being. During the 2005–2006 school year, for instance, tuition and fees at a four-year public college averaged $5,491, not including housing costs, according to The College Board.

The good news is that there's a wide range of exciting, satisfying careers available without a four-year bachelor's degree or even a two-year associate's degree. Great Careers with a High School Diploma highlights specific, in-demand careers in which individuals who have only a high school diploma or the general educational development (GED) credential can find work, with or without further training (outside of college). These jobs span the range from apprentice electronics technician to chef, teacher's assistant, Webpage designer, sales associate, and lab technician. The additional training that some of these positions require may be completed either on the job, through a certificate program, or during an apprenticeship that combines entry-level work and class time.

Happily, there's plenty of growth in the number of jobs that don't require a college diploma. That growth is fastest for positions that call for additional technical training or a certificate of proficiency. The chief economist at the Economic Policy Foundation, a think tank, notes that there are simply more of these positions available than there are workers to fill them. In fact, only 23 percent of the jobs available in the coming years will require a four-year degree or higher, the foundation reports.

It's often said that higher education is linked to higher earnings. But this is not the whole story. Correctional officer, computer network technician, and electrician are just a few of the careers that offer strong income-earning potential. What's more, the gap that exists between the wages of high school graduates and those with college degrees has begun to close slightly. Between 2000 and 2004, the yearly earnings of college graduates dropped by 5.6 percent while the earnings of high school graduates increased modestly by 1.6 percent according to the Economic Policy Foundation. High school graduates earn a median yearly income of $26,104, according the U.S. Census Bureau.

So what career should a high school graduate consider? The range is so broad that Great Careers with a High School Diploma includes 10 volumes, each based on related career fields from the Department of Labor's career clusters. Within each volume approximately 10 careers are profiled, encouraging readers to focus on a wide selection of job possibilities, some of which readers may not even know exist. To enable readers to narrow their choices, each chapter offers a self-assessment quiz that helps answer the question, "Is this career for me?" What's more, each job profile includes an insightful look at what the position involves, highlights of a typical day, insight into the work environment, and an interview with someone on the job.

An essential part of the decision to enter a particular field includes how much additional training is needed. Great Careers features opportunities that require no further academic study or training beyond high school as well as those that do. Readers in high school can start prepping for careers immediately through volunteer work, internships, academic classes, technical programs, or career academies. (Currently, for instance, one in four students concentrates on a vocational or technical program.) For each profile, the best ways for high school students to prepare are featured in a "What You Can Do Now" section.

For readers who are called to serve in the armed forces, this decision also provides an opportunity to step into a range of careers. Every branch of the armed forces from the army to the coast guard offers training in areas including administrative, construction, electronics, health care, and protective services. One volume of Great Careers with a High School Diploma is devoted to careers than can be reached with military training. These range from personnel specialist to aircraft mechanic.

Beyond military options, other entry-level careers provide job seekers with an opportunity to test-drive a career without a huge commitment. Compare the ease of switching from being a bank teller to a sales representative, for instance, with that of investing three years and tens of thousands of dollars into a law school education, only to discover a dislike for the profession. Great Careers offers not only a look at related careers, but also ways to advance in the field. Another section, "How to Find a Job," provides job-hunting tips specific to each career. This includes, for instance, advice for teacher assistants to develop a portfolio of their work. As it turns out,

employers of entry-level workers aren't looking for degrees and academic achievements. They want employability skills: a sense of responsibility, a willingness to learn, discipline, flexibility, and above all, enthusiasm. Luckily, with 100 jobs profiled in Great Careers with a High School Diploma, finding the perfect one to get enthusiastic about is easier than ever.

Work outdoors

Groundskeeper (Landscaper, Tree Trimmer)

Beautify your community

Have variety in your job

Groundskeeper *(Landscaper, Tree Trimmer)*

If you like working outside with your hands and enjoy planting flowers and trees, you might want to consider a career as a groundskeeper. Groundskeepers maintain outdoor areas such as those around public buildings, schools, offices, and residences, as well as parks, golf courses, cemeteries, and athletic fields. The work varies by climate and by season, and it involves much more than just using your hands to dig in the dirt and plant flowers. Groundskeepers also use equipment to mow lawns and prune trees and shrubs, and they sometimes paint and clear snow. If you think you might have a talent for landscape design, starting out as a groundskeeper is a good way to explore your interest and aptitude. There are about 1.5 million people working as groundskeepers or in related jobs. Most of them are Spanish-speaking immigrants. Demand for various types of landscape workers is increasing—you could say it is a growing field.

Is This Job for You?

To find out if being a groundskeeper is a good fit for you, read each of the following questions and answer "Yes" or "No."

Yes	*No*	**1.**	Do you like to work outdoors?
Yes	*No*	**2.**	Are you strong and physically fit?
Yes	*No*	**3.**	Are you or could you be comfortable using chainsaws, hedge trimmers, mowers, and other potentially dangerous equipment?
Yes	*No*	**4.**	Do you like to garden and care for trees, plants, and flowers?
Yes	*No*	**5.**	Do you work well on a small team?
Yes	*No*	**6.**	Do you speak Spanish, or are you willing to learn?
Yes	*No*	**7.**	Do you have the stamina to do physical labor all day?
Yes	*No*	**8.**	Do you *not* have seasonal allergies or would be able to manage them?
Yes	*No*	**9.**	Can you work independently with directions?
Yes	*No*	**10.**	Do you like your work to change with the seasons?

If you can answer "Yes" to most or all of these questions, read on to find out more about a career as a groundskeeper.

Let's Talk Money

Groundskeepers usually earn around $9 per hour. Experienced managers top out at around $17 an hour. The annual salary of a groundskeeper ranges from $22,000 to $30,000, depending upon your experience, location, and the type of grounds that you maintain (e.g., an elementary school versus a private estate). Tree trimmers make about $12 per hour.

What You'll Do

The duties of groundskeepers and landscapers frequently overlap, so sometimes the titles are used interchangeably. Landscapers are responsible for lawn care and maintaining flowers, trees, and other flora on a property. They plant, weed, fertilize, mow, prune, treat for pests and diseases, and generally keep green areas looking tidy and attractive. Groundskeepers are sometimes also responsible for maintaining and painting the exteriors of buildings, putting up and repairing fences, cleaning, de-icing and shoveling paved surfaces, and maintaining athletic fields, including pools and courts. Groundskeepers look after outdoor furniture, playground equipment, and other seasonal features. They pick up litter and keep their grounds neat and orderly. They usually repair and maintain all of their equipment.

Tree trimmers prune trees and shrubs using a variety of saws and clippers. Sometimes the trimming is done to keep trees and shrubs healthy or in a shape that is pleasing to the eye. Sometimes trimming is necessary to keep roadways, sidewalks, power lines, and other corridors clear from branches and overgrowth.

Who You'll Work For

- Landscaping companies
- Federal, state, and local governments
- Botanical gardens
- Cemeteries
- Golf courses
- Parks and recreation departments
- Private landscape architects, designers, and contractors
- Private schools, clubs, estates, and residences

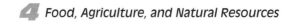

✴ Commercial and residential building complexes
✴ Colleges and universities
✴ Athletic complexes
✴ Amusement parks

Where You'll Work

Your work environment will depend on your geographic climate and the type of employer that you choose. If you work in a cemetery or memorial garden, you may dig graves, mow around graves, and pull weeds to keep the areas around gravestones tidy. If you work for a landscaping company, you will be sent out as a member of a work crew to work on their clients' properties. The clients could be commercial, such as an office complex with green spaces to mow, trees and shrubs to trim, and flowers to plant and flowerbeds to weed. The work site also could be a private residence, where you will be doing the yard work for a busy family or maybe for an elderly person who needs assistance with lawn care. If you work for the government, you could be mowing highway medians, planting flowers to beautify roadways, or you could be perched high in a cherry picker, trimming branches to keep utility lines clear.

Your schedule will change seasonally. Typically, planting occurs in the spring, followed by fertilizing and weeding through the summer. In the autumn, you might plant bulbs and mulch flowerbeds for the winter. In the winter, you may de-ice sidewalks and driveways and keep parking lots plowed. If you live in a warm climate, you may be pruning and planting all year round. Some places like to change the plants they have seasonally, so you may be removing flowers and planting new ones in different colors or patterns.

The Inside Scoop: Q&A

Keith Risley
Grounds manager
Bethesda-By-the-Sea, Palm Beach, Florida

Q: *How did you get your job?*

A: I had been working for nearly four years in a similar type of job (lawn care), and I was made aware of an opening at the Episcopal Church by some parishioners. I wanted to continue working outside (not a desk job), so I went for an interview, and was subsequently hired.

Q: *What do you like best about your job?*

A: I am a "self-starter," and I enjoy working on my own and being my own boss (other than conferring with a grounds committee at the church, I'm on my own). I like the fact that as I prune (cut back), or plant new flora, I see the results of my labors immediately. Due to the high profile nature of our Palm Beach church, the fruits of these labors are seen daily by locals and tourists. I have been able to win awards for the gardens, and it is quite nice to receive those accolades.

Q: *What's the most challenging part of your job?*

A: What challenges you most in the South Florida area is that you are at the mercy of the weather conditions. First, it is hard to find people willing to work in the heat here, as well as someone willing to put in the hours of preparation for hurricane season. Not to mention the time spent with clean up afterwards.

Q: *What are the keys to success to being a groundskeeper?*

A: Weather conditions can make you or break you . . . and when they are optimal, it allows for flora and fauna to have a good growing season and therefore creates quite a showplace for parishioners and tourists to walk through and enjoy. It is imperative to keep learning about your craft, because knowing your climate, terrain, and plant materials, and how they adapt to the environment here, is crucial, especially when your work is in the public eye on a daily basis.

Sometimes, too much or too little rain will affect your work schedule. You may have to wait for better weather to do some tasks, or your clients may need you to go around and water to keep the plants alive during dry periods.

Your Typical Day

Here are the highlights of a typical day for a groundskeeper at a landscaping company with multiple properties that it is contracted to maintain.

- ✓ **Get your assignment for the day.** Find out from your boss what property or properties you will be working on that day and meet up with the rest of your crew.
- ✓ **Prepare your equipment.** Make sure that all of the tools and safety equipment that you will need for the day's tasks are loaded onto your crew's vehicles. If you will be planting, check that you have the right number and type of plants.
- ✓ **Check over your job site before you leave.** At the end of each day, or whenever a job is finished, check that the area where you were working is left clean and neat, and that no work tools or trash are left behind.

What You Can Do Now

- ✴ Get a summer, weekend, or after-school job with a local landscaping or lawn care company. Most hire high school students, especially in the busy summer months. Working for a landscape company is the perfect way to find out if the job is for you.
- ✴ If you do not already speak Spanish, take a Spanish class at your high school. Most landscape workers speak Spanish as their first language and knowing the language will help you communicate with other members of your work crew.
- ✴ Take classes in botany and horticulture, if your high school offers them. Look for classes offered by botanical gardens or community education groups. Get books from the library to learn the names and growing conditions for plants local to your area.
- ✴ Volunteer at a community garden. Start your own garden plot or even just a window box. If you live in a suburban or rural area, offer to mow lawns and weed for neighbors. Put up signs offering your services at reasonable rates.

What Training You'll Need

Most groundskeepers and landscapers learn on the job. Some knowledge of plants is useful, but it is not a requirement to get most entry-level jobs. Some employers will not require that you have a high school diploma or GED (general educational development) credential, but it may be a prerequisite to getting certain types of certification.

You will need to learn how to handle delicate plants without damaging them, and how to plant them and care for them so that they will grow in their new locations. You will also need to learn how to prune trees and shrubs, weed flowerbeds and mow lawns. In some climates, you will have to learn to operate plows and snow blowers.

Much of your on-the-job training will involve learning how to use, maintain, and repair the tools of your trade safely. Experienced groundskeepers will teach you how to use equipment like chainsaws, trimmers, mowers, leaf blowers, and wood chippers safely and effectively in your work.

Some jobs will require you to drive your equipment to the job site, so a driver's license and a clean driving record will be essential for these jobs.

There are many certification programs for landscape professionals. Certification can increase your employability and raise your pay. (See "Web Sites to Surf" at the end of this chapter for more information.)

How to Talk Like a Pro

Here are a few words you'll hear as a groundskeeper, landscaper, or tree trimmer:

* ✰ **Greenskeeper** The name for a groundskeeper who maintains a golf course. In addition to the typical duties of a groundskeeper, a greenskeeper must move the holes around on the greens to add variety to the course, and make sure that the ball washers, tee markers, canopies, and other equipment specific to a golf course are in good repair.
* ✰ **Balled and burlapped** Also "B&B," this term refers to the root ball of a tree or shrub being wrapped in burlap for transport after it has been dug up to be transplanted to a new location.
* ✰ **Dethatching** Dethatching is the removal of a dead layer of turf-grass so that new sod can be laid down or other plantings can take place. Landscapers do a lot of dethatching.

How to Find a Job

Finding a job as a groundskeeper can be as easy as walking into the closest landscaping company and asking if they are hiring. You can also contact your local parks and recreation department. Sometimes parks, gardens, athletic fields, and other recreational facilities will have signs saying who maintains them. Call them up and tell them you are interested in working for them. You can also contact local golf courses and cemeteries to see if they are hiring entry-level laborers. Most employers will not require that you have experience, but tell them about any landscape work that you have done and convey that you are eager to learn on the job. Enthusiasm and good communication skills will impress a potential employer.

If you see a local building with good landscaping, ask the owner who does their work for them. If you see a crew out working, ask them who they work for.

Secrets for Success

See the suggestions below and turn to the appendix for advice on résumés and interviews.

* Take care in your work. Unevenly trimmed trees and shrubs, or dirt and branches left around a job site, could cost you your job—eventually. Plants that look attractive and healthy will show your boss and your clients that you are careful and that you take pride in your work.
* Learn to estimate how long it takes you to complete tasks. Your employers will appreciate this, and your workday will be calmer.

Reality Check

Landscaping work can involve long hours out in the hot sun in the summer and in the cold clearing snow in the winter. Make sure that you dress appropriately for the weather, wear sunscreen, and drink lots of water to avoid dehydration. If you are not given training in how to use the equipment you need for a job, ask. It is better to tell your boss that you have never used a chain saw or wood chipper than to fake it and wind up injured.

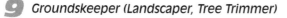

Some Other Jobs to Think About

✳ Pest-management technician. Pest-management technicians apply chemical sprays to control insects and weeds, prevent diseases, and stimulate the growth of decorative plants and crops. You could work for chemical lawn care services, farmers, golf courses, or specialized pest-control companies.

✳ Forestry worker or logger. There are a variety of jobs related to forestry that you might consider. Foresters can be involved in conservation and management of forests—or they can work for logging companies, cutting down and hauling trees.

✳ Agricultural worker. Agricultural workers perform a variety of tasks on farms and ranches, from planting and fertilizing crops to picking and packaging produce. Agricultural workers may also work with animals in the meat and dairy industries.

✳ Nursery employee. Employees of a commercial nursery grow plants that will be purchased and transplanted. They care for seedlings and advise customers on which plants to choose for their growing environment.

How You Can Move Up

✳ Become a supervisor. You can move up to a supervisory role in your job with experience and good organizational and communication skills.

✳ Become a landscape contractor by starting your own business. After you have been a supervisor for a while, you may want to strike out on your own and start your own landscape business. You will need good references to build up a client base, and have the ability to hire and train your own employees. Some states have licensing requirements for landscape contractors, so check the laws in your state.

✳ Become a landscape designer or landscape architect. If you have an interest and a talent for creating attractive landscape design plans, you may be able to get hired by clients just to do design work. It takes a four-year degree to become a certified landscape architect, but you can usually work your way through school.

✳ Become an arborist. You will need to learn about proper tree care and how to choose the right type of tree for different environments. You will supervise tree trimmers and planters.

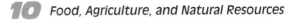

Tree Care Industry Association. This site contains everything you need to know about becoming a certified arborist. You can look up tree care companies by zip code and get information on careers in arboriculture. http://www.treecareIndustry.org

Professional Landcare Network (PLANET). PLANET provides information for both commercial and residential lawn care professionals. It offers certification exams for various categories of landscape technicians. http://www.landcarenetwork.org

Professional Grounds Management Association (PGMS). PGMS is a resource for institutional grounds managers, such as groundskeepers for colleges and universities, parks and recreation facilities, commercial and residential complexes, cemeteries, and municipalities. They provide education for professional development and certification. http://www.pgms.org

Help prevent forest fires

Forestry/ Conservation/ Logging-Crew Member

Work outdoors all year round

Join a traditional industry

Forestry/Conservation/Logging-Crew Member

One of the most important natural resources in the United States is our forests. Our nation's forests serve many functions, providing a source of natural beauty and recreation for humans, a carbon sink to cleanse the air we breathe, a habitat for wildlife, and a source of wood and other forest products. The forestry sector provides a variety of job opportunities for workers with a high school diploma. In 2004, there were about 92,000 people employed as logging equipment operators, tree fallers, forest conservation workers, and graders and scalers. Most of the work does not require education beyond the high school level as it consists mainly of operating heavy equipment, such as feller-bunchers and loaders, that you can really only learn to do on the job, not in a classroom. Logging requires a great deal of physical strength and stamina, as well as the ability to operate complicated heavy machinery with strict attention to safety.

Is This Job for You?

To find out if being a Logger is a good fit for you, read each of the following statements and answer "Yes" or "No."

Yes	*No*	**1.**	Are you willing to work outdoors in any weather?
Yes	*No*	**2.**	Do you not mind work that is physically demanding and hazardous?
Yes	*No*	**3.**	Are you willing to work in isolated areas?
Yes	*No*	**4.**	Are you comfortable operating heavy machinery, or at least willing to give it a try?
Yes	*No*	**5.**	Are you healthy, strong, and physically fit?
Yes	*No*	**6.**	Do you have a lot of stamina?
Yes	*No*	**7.**	Can you exercise good judgment?
Yes	*No*	**8.**	Are you mechanically inclined, and could you learn to maintain heavy equipment?
Yes	*No*	**9.**	Do you not mind commuting a long distance to a job site?
Yes	*No*	**10.**	Do you not mind a job that requires hard, physical labor every day?

If you can answer "Yes" to most of these questions, read on to find out more about a career in forestry.

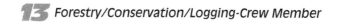

Let's Talk Money

Average hourly pay for logging and forestry conservation workers varied from $9.51–$14.29 in 2004. Larger firms usually paid higher wages, as did companies in Alaska and the Pacific Northwest. Loggers get few benefits, such as health insurance, and smaller firms might not even provide safety equipment. Government workers tend to get better benefits than those in the private sector.

What You'll Do

There are many kinds of jobs in this field. Many loggers work as tree fallers, using chain saws and falling machines to cut down trees in a forest and transport it to saw mills. But the work of a logging crew is divided into many specific jobs. Choke setters fasten steel cables and chains onto felled trees so that they can be skidded to trucks and waterways for transport. Other logging equipment operators load and unload logs at railways and sawmills. There are also rigging slingers, chasers, log sorters, markers, movers, and chippers, each with their own machinery and tasks. On a typical logging crew of four to eight members, you would be expected to learn to do several of these jobs well, including maintaining the equipment that you use.

Once the trees get to a sawmill, graders and scalers take over—using saws, and cutting and planning devices—to prepare the logs to be sold for various consumer and industrial uses. Today, there are very few sawmills operating in the United States. Most felled trees are shipped abroad to be processed because of cheaper labor; then the wood may come back to the United States to be used in construction or the paper industry or for furniture.

As a forest conservation worker, you might thin woodlands to prevent forest fires in dry areas. You also would plant seedlings to regenerate deforested areas and abate infestations of insects that damage trees. Sorting and preparing seedlings for transplanting might be part of your duties. Controlling soil erosion is another job you would have as a forest conservation worker. Soil erosion is a problem in areas that have been deforested because tree roots help hold the soil in place. Once the trees are gone, soil can wash into nearby waterways and cause problems for fish and for people who live downstream.

If you work for the government on public lands, you would also clean campsites, possibly including rest rooms and recreational facilities. You would have to clear debris from roadways around the campground and keep trails clear of encroaching underbrush. Cataloging data about forests might form part of your duties. You might take a handheld device into the woods to note the types, ages, and health of various trees and other species of flora and fauna around them. This data might be used to track endangered species, maintain forest health and species diversity, or provide information to potential buyers about what types and sizes of trees are available for logging.

It's also possible that you could work on a tree farm. Would you like to grow Christmas trees? There also are tree farms that specialize in ornamental trees or trees for specific uses, like furniture. On a tree farm, you'd be responsible for planting seedlings, controlling weeds and other pests, pruning the trees to encourage them to grow in a certain shape, and harvesting them and wrapping them for shipping. In some places, you might tap trees for syrup, or harvest mosses, pine cones, and other plant life that are found around trees. About 30 percent of forestry workers are self-employed as independent contractors.

Who You'll Work For

- ✶ USDA Forest Service
- ✶ Logging contractors
- ✶ Sawmills and planing mills
- ✶ Self
- ✶ Tree farms
- ✶ State and local government

Let's Talk Trends

Job opportunities in the forestry sector are projected to grow slower than average for the next decade. Openings in the logging industry will result mostly from attrition—the job attracts young men who often move on to less hazardous jobs as they age. Government forestry jobs concerned with preventing wildfires may grow slightly, but the increasing mechanization of the timber harvesting industry, along with cheaper foreign labor, are likely to result in more layoffs than jobs in the private sector for the foreseeable future.

Where You'll Work

You'll spend most of your time working outdoors, unless you happen to work in a sawmill or planing mill. In the north, most logging is done in the winter because the frozen ground makes it easier to move the logs. Logging can also be done in very dry weather, but rain and mud can cause delays to the extent that you may have to find other work during the off-season. Loggers frequently have to travel a long way to get to their job sites, and some even stay in bunkhouses. But it depends upon the area in which you live, so don't let that discourage you from looking.

Your Typical Day

Here are the highlights for a typical day for a forest conservation worker working for a private timber company, although most of these tasks would be the same if you were working for the government.

- ✔ **Trim or cut down diseased trees.** Using hand tools like chain saws, cut down trees that have been marked as diseased or otherwise undesirable and remove them from the site.
- ✔ **Spray trees with pesticides.** If insects or fungi are attacking the trees, you may be asked to spray them with insecticides and fungicides. You might also spray herbicides on the undergrowth to ensure that other vegetation there does not compete with the trees for light and nutrients in the soil. Make sure that you wear protective equipment, which may include a breathing mask, even if your employer does not require it or provide it.
- ✔ **Perform duties assigned by professional forester.** These may include examining trees and doing such tasks as measuring them, marking them, and counting them. You might be asked to conduct controlled burns of underbrush or boundary areas, or to mark boundary lines with paint.

What You Can Do Now

Look up information on forestry-related careers and conservation on the Internet or at your local library. There is a lot of research you can do now to help narrow down the area where you might like to work.

- ✭ The USDA Forest Service has an unpaid internship program for high school students. Learn more about it here: http://www.fs.fed.us/fsjobs/forestservice/other.html

✳ A summer job in a nursery now can help you land a forestry-related job later. And many nurseries are happy to hire high school students to perform manual labor in the busy spring and summer seasons. Ask around at your local nurseries.

✳ Christmas tree sellers often hire high school kids to help sell trees between Thanksgiving and Christmas.

What Training You'll Need

As stated above, most of your training will be on the job, learning to operate expensive equipment that is used just for the logging industry. When you start out as a logging-crew member, you will be given less-skilled work, such as clearing brush.

Some vocational and technical schools offer two-year degree courses in fields such as conservation and forest harvesting. There are also training programs in most states that lead to logger certification. A degree or certificate that includes both classroom and field work might give you an edge in a dwindling job market.

How to Talk Like a Pro

Here are a few terms of the trade:

✳ **Dibble bars and hoedads** These are the funny names for digging and planting tools that are used to plant tree seedlings.

✳ **Buckers** *Buck* means cut, and buckers are members of a logging crew who use chain saws to trim off tree tops and branches and cut logs into shorter lengths.

✳ **Chokers** Chokers are steel cables or chains that are attached to felled trees in order to skid (drag) them to the roadway so that they can be sorted and put on trucks.

How to Find a Job

In order to find a job as a logger, you should look to the World Wide Web for leads on job openings in your area. There are many state and regional logging trade associations, and they usually list local job openings on their Web sites. The Associated Oregon Loggers is the largest in the country (http://www.oregonloggers.org) but, if you live

The Inside Scoop: Q&A

Justin Kennick
Logger
Northampton, Massachusetts

Q: *How did you get your job?*

A: I started working with my brother in the fire-wood business back in 1976. There was a lot of work available back then, mostly chain saw work. People were desperate for help then.

Q: *What do you like best about your job?*

A: I really like working outdoors. I like the sense of accomplishment—you can actually see what you have gotten done. I love to watch a load of logs leave the landing and know that I cut every one of them.

Q: *What's the most challenging part of your job?*

A: There are so many variables in logging. There are changes in the weather, changes in ground conditions, changes in the equipment that you have to learn to use, and changes in the market for forest products.

Q: *What are the keys to success to being a logger?*

A: You have to be willing to work physically and mentally. You have to be respectful with other people's equipment and respectful of the forest or you won't be logging for very long.

in another area with an active forest resources industry, a quick search should find an association near you. Many logging contractors are independent businessmen with small crews that they hire seasonally for logging jobs. For these employers, you may be expected to provide your own safety equipment and have some experience using chain saws and other equipment. The way to find out is to ask local contractors if they are willing to take you on and train you. The same goes for sawmills and planing mills. If there is one where you live, walk in and ask the foreman if he is hiring. It never hurts to introduce yourself and ask if there are any jobs available.

About 45 percent of all forestry workers are employed by the government so checking local, state, or federal government Web sites for job listings is a good place to start, especially if you are interested in conservation rather than timber processing.

Secrets for Success

See the suggestions below and turn to the appendix for advice on résumés and interviews.

⭐ Be safety conscious. Remember, logging is the second most hazardous job in the United States. Make sure that you wear a hardhat, eye protection, and—especially important—ear protection, as the noise from the machinery and the falling trees can damage your hearing over time. You will also need to wear tough boots. If you are doing a controlled burn, you will have to be super careful about containing the fire and not getting burned or inhaling smoke. Finally, you will need to follow all necessary safety precautions when handling pesticides.

⭐ Earn the trust and respect of your colleagues through hard work and honest dealing.

Reality Check

Logging is one of the most dangerous jobs. It ranks number two in the annual statistics of deaths per 100,000 workers, second only to fishing workers. Think seriously about the risks involved in this line of work before you decide that logging is the career for you.

Some Other Jobs to Think About

⭐ Grounds maintenance worker. These laborers look after the landscaping in a variety of settings. The work is not highly skilled, or highly paid, but it varies seasonally and you could work at college campuses, golf courses, sports facilities, corporate office complexes, malls, schools, parks, private homes, and anyplace else with landscaping that must be trimmed, planted, watered, and otherwise maintained. (See Chapter 1 for more information.)

⭐ Material moving operators. These workers use heavy equipment to move earth, debris, construction materials, and other stuff that weighs too much to lift by hand. This job involves operating large machinery, and the work can vary seasonally. Demand for these workers is high, and you can train on the job. Although the pay averages only around $13 per hour, it is higher for those workers who learn to operate specialized equipment such as cranes and pumps.

✴ Forest ranger or firefighter. Forest rangers patrol forests to make sure that people using the forests for recreation are safe and following all rules about campfires, trash disposal, vehicle use, etc. Firefighters put out forest fires and try to prevent fires from spreading to developed areas.

How You Can Move Up

✴ As you gain experience and prove your reliability and skill, you are likely to be given increased responsibilities. If you ask to learn how to use more sophisticated and specialized equipment, you may become able to supervise other loggers and train new ones. You might specialize in one phase of timber processing, and spend most of your time operating the equipment for that task. You might even decide to work for a company, such as John Deere, that makes logging equipment, and go around demonstrating it and training workers in how to use it.

✴ In the area of conservation, you could go to school and get a four-year degree in conservation biology or forestry. A degree would open up a whole new range of level forestry jobs for you, at higher pay and with benefits.

Web Sites to Surf

Society of American Foresters. This site contains lots of information about careers in forestry, including a special section just for students. http://www.safnet.org

Forest Resources Association, Inc. This organization provides information about the forest products industry and lists programs that offer training for logging-related occupations. http://www.forestresources.org

USDA Forest Service. Federal government Web site contains detailed maps and information about national forests by state and name, as well as job listings. http://www.fs.fed.us

Make living plants your living

Nursery/ Greenhouse Assistant

Turn your green thumb into a livelihood

Nurture the next generation of vegetation

Nursery/Greenhouse Assistant

When you are outside, look around and you are likely to see grass, trees, shrubs, and flowers. They may be in the yards of homeowners, or in the landscaping borders that add a bit of cheerful nature to schools, office buildings, apartment complexes, hospitals, and other developments. These plants do not usually go into the ground as seeds. More often, seedlings are grown in commercial nurseries and greenhouses and, when they have reached a certain size, the plants are purchased and transplanted into their new homes. Nursery and greenhouse assistants are the people who grow these plants from seeds, and then sell them to individuals and businesses.

Is This Job for You?

To find out if being a nursery/greenhouse assistant is a good fit for you, read each of the following statements and answer "Yes" or "No."

Yes	No	**1.**	Have you been told that you have a "green thumb," and do you enjoy growing things?
Yes	No	**2.**	Do you not mind getting wet and dirty on a job?
Yes	No	**3.**	Are you willing to do physical labor all day at your workplace?
Yes	No	**4.**	Can you tolerate working with pesticides, herbicides and fungicides?
Yes	No	**5.**	Can you see yourself digging in dirt all day long?
Yes	No	**6.**	Do you not mind being on your feet all day, and doing some heavy lifting?
Yes	No	**7.**	Would you enjoy helping customers choose plants that are appropriate for their homes and businesses?
Yes	No	**8.**	Would you like to learn how to take care of many different types of plants?
Yes	No	**9.**	Can you carefully handle delicate plants, such as seedlings?
Yes	No	**10.**	Do you like the idea of helping things grow?

If you can answer "Yes" to most of these questions, read on to find out more about a career in the nursery business.

Let's Talk Money

Nursery and greenhouse work is extremely low paying. The average hourly rate in 2004 was $7.70 per hour. Nursery and greenhouse workers are rarely unionized. Some jobs come with benefits, including health and retirement savings accounts. Jobs in rural areas tend to come with housing; jobs in urban areas are less likely to offer housing as part of the compensation package.

What You'll Do

Nursery and greenhouse workers function as the parents of commercially grown plants. They raise them from seeds and then send them out into the world. You will have the satisfaction of seeing seeds that you planted in tiny flats sprout and grow into sturdy plants that you will then have to transplant into larger containers. Each day, you will water, fertilize, prune, weed, and otherwise tend to your assigned plants. You may care for flowers, vines, shrubs, trees, or other flora. Some nurseries and greenhouses specialize in one type of plant, such as roses. A greenhouse full of roses smells wonderful and looks beautiful. Greenhouses are also used to grow out-of-season fruits and vegetables or to grow them in a climate that would not sustain them outdoors. So you might be tending strawberries in a greenhouse in December, watching snow fall outside the warm glass. Occasionally, plants are grown hydroponically, that is, in nutrient-rich water instead of soil. These plants require slightly different care, which you would learn on the job.

The work you will do may seem repetitive at times as you may have many rows of identical plants, all in the same stage of growth and all needing the same type of attention. You'll need to exercise great care in handling delicate plants, especially during the transplanting phase when they are most vulnerable.

If you deal directly with customers, you will need to be knowledgeable about what types of plants will grow best in that customer's type of soil and climate. You'll need to ask questions such as how much shade the proposed planting area has and what type of drainage. The more you know about ideal growing conditions for your plants, the more satisfied your customers will be.

Let's Talk Trends

Although agricultural jobs in general are expected to decline for the foreseeable future, nursery and greenhouse job opportunities are likely to increase. This is because the need for landscaping is offsetting farm consolidation and the technological advances that are causing other agricultural jobs to decline. Job turnover is high due to low pay and poor working conditions, making it relatively easy to get a job.

Who *You'll Work For*

- ✗ Commercial nurseries
- ✗ Commercial greenhouses
- ✗ Specialty greenhouses and nurseries such as rose growers
- ✗ Commercial hydroponic greenhouses
- ✗ Nursery sections of major retailers
- ✗ Small, family-owned nurseries and greenhouses
- ✗ University research departments
- ✗ Agricultural product packing and shipping companies

Where *You'll Work*

Your job environment will depend on many factors, including the type of employer you choose, whether large or small, the climate in your geographic location, and the types of plants grown in the nursery or greenhouse where you are employed. If you tend trees or shrubs, you will probably be working outdoors. If you tend delicate plants in a cold climate, you will be working in a greenhouse that is heated to a temperature much warmer than the outside air.

Your workplace will also vary by size. Huge commercial growers can have multiple, cavernous greenhouses on one site, with hundreds of workers, whereas a mom-and-pop nursery may have only one or two small greenhouses, a few rows of trees and shrubs out back, and a few employees.

The biggest difference in your work environment will depend upon whether you grow food or decorative plants, and whether or not you sell directly to the public. If you grow food, you may have little to do at certain phases of its growth but then you may have to work long hours harvesting and packing your produce when it is just ripe. If you sell directly to the public, you may need additional training in plant selection, and you are more likely to work for a business that sells a variety of decorative plants rather than a monoculture enterprise.

Finally, universities and agricultural corporations employ greenhouse assistants in their research departments. These workers tend plants that are grown for experiments on plant genetics, pesticide resistance, and many other purposes. This can be an exciting environment if you are interested in science.

Your Typical Day

Here are the highlights for a typical day for a greenhouse assistant working for a large, commercial greenhouse.

- ✔ **Prepare soil for planting.** Using gardening tools, mix soil so that it has the appropriate nutrients, density, and acidity for your seeds. Fill each compartment of large planting trays with the soil.
- ✔ **Plant seeds.** Place appropriate number of seeds in each compartment in your flats, at the depth needed for that particular seed to sprout.
- ✔ **Water plants and check irrigation equipment.** Your newly planted seeds will need to be watered right away. Then, you will need to check the irrigation system in your greenhouse to make sure that it releases the appropriate amount of water or mist, at the correct intervals, for your plants.

What You Can Do Now

- ✴ Get an after-school, weekend, or summer job at a local greenhouse or nursery. Some nurseries hire high school students to help sell Christmas trees, wreaths, and other greenery during the holiday season.
- ✴ If your high school offers any plant-related science classes, take them. Look around for classes in your community as well.
- ✴ Get a driver's license and maintain a clean driving record. Some jobs will require driving and potential employers will look at your driving history.

The Inside Scoop: Q&A

**Laurie Kasperek
Greenhouse Assistant, Biology Department,
Binghamton University—State University
of New York, Binghamton, New York**

Q: *How did you get your job?*

A: At the entry level positions (retail greenhouse businesses), I was chosen for the job due to having some plant-culture
background, primarily through the cooperative extension's Master
Gardener Program. As I moved up in the green industry, I was
chosen for management positions based on higher education in
plant science, internships at a public garden, and holding a license
as a Commercial Pesticide Applicator.

Q: *What do you like best about your job?*

A: I like working in an environment that brings great joy to visitors
of the collections in the teaching greenhouse. As I moved up, the
levels the responsibilities increased, but so did the ability to set my
own priorities and workday.

Q: *What's the most challenging part of your job?*

A: Entry-level retail positions come with the challenges of dealing
with many different customers; and patience, diplomacy, cheerful-
ness, and self-assurance are all necessary to get through the day.
The hours may be on weekends and holidays, making your own
family gatherings come second. Many duties can become routine
very rapidly.

Q: *What are the keys to success to being a greenhouse
assistant?*

A: The most important key has been to seek continuing education,
thus putting me in a position to move from retail jobs to acade-
mia, where there is a chance to tailor my work to my personality
and goals.

What Training You'll Need

Although you can get a job at a nursery or greenhouse with a high school degree, some technical colleges offer Nursery/Greenhouse Technician certificate programs that may give you an edge in getting a job. These programs will teach you such skills as plant identification, pest control, fertilizer use, irrigation techniques, garden center management, and even greenhouse design, construction, and maintenance. Some sort of certification is usually necessary to move up to a supervisory position. In some cases, your employer may be willing to pay for this training—it never hurts to ask.

To figure out what training is most appropriate for you, consider where you might work. The skills needed to grow dwarf varieties of trees outdoors are somewhat different from those needed to grow red peppers hydroponically indoors. In either case, you will be trained on the job. The most important training you can have prior to finding employment is in how to follow directions. Your work will be largely independent, but you will need to follow instructions, especially when you are new to the job and cannot yet judge from experience whether plants need pruning or watering, or if they are ready to be transplanted. It also helps if you are self-motivated as you may be working with little supervision.

How to Talk Like a Pro

Here are a few terms of the trade:

- ✴ **Hydroponics** A system of growing plants in nutrient-enriched water instead of soil.
- ✴ **pH** pH is a measurement of the concentration of hydrogen ions in soil, fertilizer, or irrigation water. The higher the pH, the more alkaline the solution. A lower pH indicates a more acidic solution. Different plants require different pH levels to thrive. The acidic soil in which a pine tree grows, for example, will kill most other plants.
- ✴ **Horticulturist** Someone who works in plant propagation, doing research into plant physiology and biochemistry with the goal of improving crop yields, transportability, and appearance.

How to Find a Job

Finding a job as a greenhouse or nursery assistant is relatively easy since most of the training occurs on the job. Employers will usually hire high school graduates, or candidates with a GED (general educational development) credential, without experience. If you have appropriate certification, you will be eligible for a higher-level job, at higher rates of pay, but don't be shy about applying for an entry-level job before you have any credentials. You can gain valuable experience at the same time you are earning certification.

Greenhouse and nursery jobs may be advertised in your local paper, but you can also just walk into local businesses and ask if they are hiring. University jobs will most likely be advertised on the university's Web site. Check for employment listings in the human resources section. You can also make contact with greenhouse managers at local universities directly and ask them to keep you in mind when they have an opening. If they get funding for a research project and find themselves in need of assistants, they may give you a call. Present yourself to potential employers as dependable and willing to follow directions. Show an interest in plants and a willingness and enthusiasm to learn quickly.

Secrets for Success

See the suggestions below and turn to the appendix for advice on résumés and interviews.

* Keep upgrading your skills. If you are motivated to study plant science at the college level, obtain certification as a nursery technician, or get licensed as a pesticide applicator, you will be able to command a higher wage and move up to management roles.
* Pay close attention to detail—those plants aren't just fragile, they cost money!

Reality Check

Agricultural jobs, including nursery and greenhouse work, are generally low-paying. This is due to the fact that entry-level jobs require few skills. In some areas, agricultural jobs are held mainly by immigrants whose lack of education and inability to speak English prevents them from obtaining higher-paying jobs.

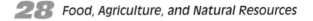

Some Other Jobs to Think About

⭐ Grounds maintenance worker. These laborers look after landscaping in a variety of settings. The work is not highly skilled, or
highly paid, but it varies seasonally and you could work at college campuses, golf courses, sports facilities, corporate office
complexes, malls, schools, parks, private homes, and anyplace
else with landscaping that must be trimmed, planted, watered,
and otherwise maintained. (See Chapter 1 for more information.)

⭐ Farm worker/agricultural technician. These laborers plant, nurture, harvest, and pack produce on large commercial farms. (See
Chapter 5 for more information.)

⭐ Forest, conservation, or logging worker. This field involves working in managed forests to cut and haul trees for commercial
uses. It is also possible to work for government agencies such as
the USDA Forest Service overseeing the condition of state and
national forests. (See Chapter 2 for more information.)

How You Can Move Up

⭐ As you gain experience and prove your reliability, you may be
given increased responsibilities. But you may find your work becoming routine and there may be a limit to how much your duties
can change if you do not obtain additional education and training.
Find out if your employer will pay all or part of the cost of a one-
year certificate program at a technical college or a two-year associate's degree in plant sciences at a community college. Also find
out if there is demand in your area for workers with specific licensing such as pesticide application. Some four-year colleges
have programs that will allow you to work full or part-time while
earning your degree, and your employer may pay for your studies.

Web Sites to Surf

American Nursery and Landscape Association. This is a membership organization that provides information on education and research. It follows legal developments related to the professions and lobbies on behalf of its members. http://www.anla.org

Colorado Nursery and Greenhouse Association. Like similar organizations in states throughout the country, this Colorado association offers valuable information about the specifics of the industry in its area. Look for the industry associations in your state. http://www.coloradonga.org

Fight wildfires

Forest Firefighter/ Range Aide

Work for the government—outdoors!

Take a stand on forest health

Forest Firefighter/Range Aide

Wilderness takes care of itself. Trees die and decay, and new saplings sprout. Insects, fungi, and bacteria feed on both dead and living tree matter. Lightning strikes cause fires that may burn huge swaths of forest, which then slowly regenerate, with new green seedlings poking up through the charred, dead wood. But life in an orchard, tree farm, or state forest is quite different. A fire is a disaster, which can cause danger to nearby houses or burn down orchard trees that supply someone's livelihood. Likewise, infestations by insects can be economically devastating. These types of managed woodlands require the availability of forest firefighters, as well as forestry aides to assist professional foresters or tree farmers in maintaining the health of their managed forest or orchard.

Is This Job for You?

To find out if being a forest firefighter/range aide is a good fit for you, read each of the following statements and answer "Yes" or "No."

Yes No **1.** Are you willing to work outdoors in any weather?

Yes No **2.** Do you mind work that is physically demanding and hazardous?

Yes No **3.** Are you willing to work in isolated areas, far from city and town?

Yes No **4.** Are you comfortable operating heavy machinery, or are you willing to give it a try?

Yes No **5.** Are you healthy, strong, and physically fit?

Yes No **6.** Do you have a lot of stamina?

Yes No **7.** Can you exercise good judgment?

Yes No **8.** Do you have a desire to fight fires, and do you fully understand the risks of this job?

Yes No **9.** Do you mind commuting a long distance to your job site?

Yes No **10.** Do you not mind a job that requires hard, physical labor every day?

If you can answer "Yes" to most of these questions, read on to find out more about a career in the field of forestry.

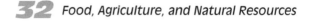

Let's Talk Money

Forestry aides make an average of $9.51 per hour. Firefighters make considerably more money. It is one of the better paying professions for entrants with only a high school degree. The median hourly earnings of firefighters in 2004 were $18.43. Pay rises with seniority, and firefighters are always paid overtime. The job also comes with benefits and a pension.

What You'll Do

As a forestry aide, you may work under the supervision of a professional forester, performing such duties as thinning woodlands to prevent forest fires in dry areas. You also would plant seedlings to regenerate deforested areas and abate infestations of insects that dry out trees and make them more susceptible to conflagration. Your work will overlap with that of a forest conservation worker, so you might want to look at Chapter 2 for more information on possible duties.

There is a big difference in what work you would perform as a forestry aide in a national or state forest and in an orchard. Trees on a tree farm are grown and maintained as monoculture crops, so the ecosystem resembles that of a field of corn more than a wild forest. Irrigation systems are sometimes employed to maintain moisture levels, and agrichemicals are applied to keep away pests and disease. Fire prevention would not be your primary concern, as it would in a natural forest.

In a state or national park, you might drive around and make sure that campers and other recreational users of the park are obeying the rules. In some places, campfires will be forbidden; in others, there will be rules for putting out fires safely. It will be your job to see that campers adhere to these rules. You also would watch for signs of smoke while out on patrol. Quick intervention is necessary to prevent a forest fire from getting out of control.

When a blaze does occur, local firefighters are brought in to contain it. If they are unsuccessful, firefighters from other regions are flown in. A very large forest fire can involve firefighters from around the country. Firefighters who battle wildfires employ different methods from those used against fires in buildings. Helicopters and airplanes are used to drop water and flame retardant chemicals on the

fire from above. Controlled fires are deliberately set in the fire's path to create a fire break to stop the blaze from progressing. Firefighters travel ahead of the blaze, anticipating which way it will move next and evacuating residents in its path.

Who You'll Work For

✯ USDA Forest Service
✯ Municipal fire departments
✯ State governments
✯ Privately owned forests

Where You'll Work

Your job environment will vary by climate and by type of employer. If you are a forestry aide for a national or state forest, you will spend most of your time outside engaged in fire prevention activities and maintenance work. You may drive a vehicle on patrol, or find yourself stationed at a particular lookout post. Your job may involve interaction with visitors, and it may involve keeping records of what you have seen and done during your workday.

If you are a firefighter for the USDA Forest Service, you will work outside fighting wildfires that are burning trees or brush. Your work may take you into different climates and terrains; the area may be flat, but it most likely will be steep. You will be working along the edges of inhabited areas, creating fire lines and breaks to prevent the spread of fires into areas with dwellings and other manmade things.

Let's Talk Trends

Although overall employment prospects in the forest sector are expected to increase more slowly than average, forestry jobs that relate to the prevention of forest fires may be an exception, particularly in areas with drier climates, and any areas where residential building is encroaching on habitat that is prone to destructive fires.

Firefighters can expect to see faster than average job growth, but this trend is somewhat offset by the keen competition for jobs. Fire fighting is a popular occupational choice for people with only a high school degree due to its challenge, importance, respect, high pay, and guaranteed pension.

You might also work as a municipal firefighter. In this case, your work environment will consist of your fire station, until you are called to put out a fire or perform some type of rescue operation. Municipal firefighters are called to assist with wildfires, but their primary task is putting out fires in buildings. If you live in an urban area, your opportunities for working on wildfires may be few and far between. If you live in a municipality that is adjacent to wildfire-prone areas, fighting wildfires may constitute a major part of your duties.

Firefighters work long shifts and are often required to work on holidays. Some departments arrange shifts in a 24 hours on–48 hours off schedule. Others have 10–14 hour day or night shifts for three to four days or nights in a row, followed by three to four days off, and then the cycle repeats.

Regardless of your schedule, or where you work, one thing that is common to all fire fighting jobs in the protective gear that you have to wear. It is hot and incredibly heavy, something that you will have to get used to.

Your Typical Day

Here are the highlights for a typical day for a USDA Forest Service firefighter.

✓ **Report to the fire station and wait.** When your shift starts, you need to be at the fire station. If you are not called to any fires, you may stay there, cleaning, inspecting equipment, engaging in practice drills, playing cards, cooking, napping, or watching television, for your entire shift.

✓ **Inspect your gear and get it ready.** If you are called to a fire, you need to be able to get to it with all possible speed. Your equipment must be in working order and set out, ready to go in an instant. Your boots are literally set beside the engine, waiting for you to step into them as you climb on board.

✓ **Receive orders on how to tackle the fire.** If your unit is called to a fire during your shift, you will need to listen to the orders of your superiors. Once you have experience fighting fires for many years, you will be the one giving the orders. You may be asked to attack the fires with water, dig a fire line, burn a fire break, evacuate residents, provide back-up support to other units, or any number of other related tasks.

The Inside Scoop: Q&A

Dana Meier
Forest firefighter
San Diego, California

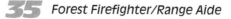

Q: *How did you get your job?*

A: I took fire science and EMT (emergency medical technician) classes at the junior college, went to fire stations to learn more about the job, and put myself in the best physical shape I could. I applied for two cities and literally had to stand in line with approximately 7,500 others for over 24 hours for one of them. After the application was accepted, we took a written exam on general common sense, learning abilities, mechanical aptitude, math, spelling, etc. Those who scored in the top group were allowed to take the physical abilities exam. This consisted of pulling hose, dry and charged, carrying and raising ladders, carrying hose, running stairs, pulling hose from the fourth story, and correctly lifting heavy objects and running with them. It was a timed event of doing all sections consecutively to test strength, abilities, and endurance.

Those who passed this exam were then interviewed. I took classes on how to take an interview, and also did mock practice interviews with other firefighters. I tried to get criticism from several different people, from those who were supportive of me and also from those who were against women in the fire service. This way I could be more prepared for the actual interview regardless of who was giving it. After approximately two years of classes, exams, and interviews, I was selected for an academy of 12 people. The academy was stressful and rigorous, and looking back now, it was great fun. But at the time, I think most were extremely stressed. Three people failed but made it almost to the very end before they did. Several were injured during the academy, one severely. Once on the job, we were put on a training crew for several months, then allowed out into the ranks as a probationary firefighter. Written critiques after every shift were put in our files. After three annual exams, we would receive a promotion to

(Continued on next page)

(continued from previous page)

firefighter 2 and be allowed to work on a promotion to the next level or for a specialty, like Hazardous Materials, EOD, etc.

Q: *What do you like best about your job?*

A: I loved the teamwork, the camaraderie, the continuous training to better ourselves. I loved being hands-on with helping people, and the excitement of fighting fires. It is a very important job, and one has to want to do their very best at all times to do well.

Q: *What's the most challenging part of your job?*

A: For me as a woman in the fire service, the most challenging part personally was acceptance by those I was working with. Each day you can work with a new crew member who is not open and accepting of anyone who is not "one of them." So these days usually started out a little stressful. But after a few calls, all would be just fine.

Q: *What are the keys to success to being a firefighter?*

A: The most important part of the job is continually learning a newer and better and safer way to handle each type of situation. Everything from helping people with life-threatening contagious diseases, to a faster safer rescue technique for extricating someone from a very dangerous situation, to learning how to recognize the signs of a hazardous material, to bombs.

What You Can Do Now

✭ Work out. This is a job that requires you to be in top physical condition, with exceptional strength, stamina, coordination, and agility. Running and lifting weights are both good activities to improve your fitness.

✭ Take courses in fire science or emergency medicine at your local community college. Any related coursework that you have completed will help your application stand out from the crowd.

✭ Study for the exam. The higher your score, the better your chances of getting an appointment. Use the Web sites at the end of the chapter to get information on how to prepare for the exam.

What Training You'll Need

In order to become a firefighter, you need to undergo a long application and training process. The first step is a written exam. This is followed by rigorous test of physical strength, stamina, coordination, and agility that simulate situations you would encounter on the job, such as carrying a fire hose up many flights of stairs or evacuating an overweight person from a burning building. You also will have to undergo a medical examination, and drug screening. Random drug screening will continue throughout your employment.

The applicants with the highest scores have the best chance of being accepted into the department's training program. You can bolster your chances by taking community college courses in fire science, emergency medicine, or hazardous materials handling.

If you are successful in getting an appointment, the next step will be attending your department's training academy. Like the exam, this will be an arduous weeding out process. You will spend time in both the classroom and on practical training learning both fire prevention and fire fighting techniques, how to handle hazardous materials, and local building codes. Firefighter trainees also must study emergency procedures, first aid, and CPR (cardiopulmonary resuscitation). All firefighters must have at least EMT-Basic certification. Some larger departments are now requiring paramedic certification. If you can get this certification on your own before you apply, you will have an advantage over other applicants. For the more practical side of your training, you will learn to use standard firefighting equipment, such as ladders, hoses, fire extinguishers, chain saws, axes, and rescue equipment.

After your basic training, you will be assigned to a fire company for a probationary period. Your training will continue here under a four-year apprenticeship program. Your on-the-job training will be supplemented with formal instruction in fire fighting techniques, equipment usage, hazardous chemical and building materials, emergency medicine, and fire prevention and safety.

As you get more experience, you will be able to take advantage of local advanced training programs and sessions administered by the U.S. National Fire Academy. These sessions will help you develop leadership skills such as management, disaster preparedness, and fire safety education. Also your department may provide tuition reimbursement for two- or four-year degrees in fire science or fire engineering. Advanced training may lead to higher pay and the opportunity to move up the ranks.

Promotion is usually dependent upon performance on written examinations and simulations of fire fighting scenarios at assessment centers. The best candidates for promotion are carefully screened and a bachelor's degree in fire science or a related field, or associate's degree from the National Fire Academy, may be necessary for positions above battalion chief.

Formal training is not the only prerequisite to being a firefighter. There are also personal qualities that are essential for this demanding job. You and other members of your crew will depend upon one another in dangerous situations. Above all, you must exercise good judgment and alertness, self-discipline, endurance, and courage. You must be strong, coordinated, agile, and have mechanical aptitude. In addition, it is essential that higher-ranking officers exhibit leadership qualities. They engage in public speaking, management, budgeting and public relations, so an aptitude for and willingness to learn these skills is compulsory.

How to Talk Like a Pro

Here are a few terms of the trade:

- ✯ **Nomex** A special flame-retardant material used to make the clothing worn by firefighters.
- ✯ **Pulaski** A standard wildfire fighting tool that looks like a combination of an axe and a hoe. A Pulaski is used for digging fire lines and cutting through tree roots.
- ✯ **Ladder fire** When fire-burning foliage on the forest floor jumps into the tree branches, this is called a ladder fire.

How to Find a Job

The majority of forestry-related jobs are in the western part of the country, where most national and private forests are located. The main employer in this field is the USDA Forest Service. There are also jobs to be found working in state and private forests. Check your state government's Web site and search the Internet for information on large forests where you live. For firefighting opportunities it is best to check with towns and cities in your area. Experience from volunteer work can be invaluable in landing you first paying position.

Secrets for Success

See the suggestions below and turn to the appendix for advice on résumés and interviews.

✯ Keep your skills up to date. The way that we prepare for and attempt to prevent disasters such as fires, hazardous materials spills, infestations, and other emergencies is continually changing. Advances in technology, psychology, criminology, and biology may affect the options available to you and the decisions that you make. It is essential that you regularly attend training sessions to update your skills.

✯ Be courteous and thoughtful toward your colleagues—information and teamwork are very important to forestry work.

Reality Check

Firefighting is an intense, physically demanding, and dangerous occupation. As this career guide went to press in 2007, four firefighters were burned to death when their engine was engulfed in flames as they battled a forest fire in Palm Springs, California. A fifth firefighter was on life support after suffering severe burns.

Some Other Jobs to Think About

✯ Emergency medical technician (EMT). Formerly called "paramedics," EMTs are trained in emergency medicine. They respond to 911 calls and accompany firefighters to fires. This job requires professional certification and a strong stomach. You must also be physically strong, as you will have to lift people and heavy equipment.

✯ Forest conservation worker. Forest conservation workers perform a variety of duties related to maintaining forest health or maintaining roads, campsites, and other facilities for human use. This occupation is virtually identical to that of forestry aide. (See Chapter 2 for more information.)

How You Can Move Up

✯ The next step up from being a forestry aide would be to become a professional forester. Many colleges, as well as vocational and technical schools, offer training programs in forestry, conservation, and wildlife management.

✷ The profession of fire fighting has a clear hierarchical line of promotion going from engineer to lieutenant, then captain, battalion chief, assistant chief, deputy chief, and, at the top, chief. While experience and examination results used to be the main criteria for promotion, fire departments are increasingly looking for a bachelor's degree in fire science or a related field for promotion above the battalion chief level.

Web Sites to Surf

International Association of firefighters. Organization that represents firefighters in the United States and Canada.   http://www.iaff.org

U.S. Fire Administration. Training and education information for firefighters. http://www.usfa.fema.gov

USDA Forest Service. Federal government Web site that contains detailed maps and information about national forests by state and name, as well as job listings.   http://www.fs.fed.us

Find work with ease

Farm Worker

Work outdoors—anywhere there are farms

Be essential to the food supply

Farm Worker

Do you ever look at the produce in your local supermarket and wonder where it comes from? Probably not. Most of us take it for granted that fresh fruits and vegetables appear on our local store shelves year round as if by magic. Actually, a tremendous amount of effort goes into planting, growing, picking, packing, and shipping every single apple, spinach leaf, strawberry, and grape. Farm workers spend all day in fields, their work changing with the seasons as they plant seeds, fertilize them, irrigate them, then help them grow by using agrichemicals to keep pests away. When the fruit or vegetable is ready to make the trip to your local supermarket, farm workers harvest it and prepare it for transport on trucks and airplanes. The work is very hard, and the pay is low, but jobs are always available. With immigration and health care reform topping the political agenda in the run-up to the 2008 U.S. presidential election, the essential role of so-called illegal immigrants in the national economy—many of whom work in farm labor—has entered mainstream discourse, possibly heralding an improvement of their working conditions and negotiating power.

Is This Job for You?

To find out if being a farm worker is a good fit for you, read each of the following statements and answer "Yes" or "No."

Yes	No	**1.**	Do you mind working outdoors in hot weather?
Yes	No	**2.**	Can you be careful in working with farm chemicals?
Yes	No	**3.**	Can you begin working at the minimum wage?
Yes	No	**4.**	Is it okay with you for your work to vary seasonally?
Yes	No	**5.**	It's important to you that your work is easy to get?
Yes	No	**6.**	Do you speak Spanish, or are you willing to learn?
Yes	No	**7.**	Is it okay that your job not come with benefits?
Yes	No	**8.**	Do you prefer working outside with your hands more than being inside an office or factory?
Yes	No	**9.**	Can you carefully handle delicate, ripening fruit?
Yes	No	**10.**	Do you like the idea of helping things grow?

If you can answer "Yes" to most of these questions, read on to find out more about a career as a farm worker.

Let's Talk Money

Agricultural work is extremely low paying. The average hourly rate for farm workers in 2004 was $7.70 per hour. Farm workers are rarely unionized and jobs rarely come with benefits, such as health insurance and retirement savings accounts. Jobs in rural areas tend to come with housing; jobs near urban areas are less likely to offer housing as part of the compensation package.

What You'll Do

Farm workers play a crucial role in ensuring that your local supermarket can stock fresh fruits and vegetables. Food grown and harvested by farm workers also finds its way into restaurant kitchens and prepared foods. Your work in this field will depend upon the type of crop that you grow and the climate in which you live. The duties of a farm worker who tends orange groves in Florida will differ from those of a farm worker who grows potatoes in Idaho.

There are certain features of the job that are consistent across regions and crops. The work is always seasonal and cyclical requires a lot of stamina. Whatever the crop being sown, the soil usually must be tilled first, the fruit or vegetable planted, the field irrigated and fertilized, and the crop tended carefully to eradicate weeds and pests. It is a lot of work! Most farm workers start their workday at sunrise and finish at sunset in order to take advantage of all available daylight. This means that you will be traveling to and from work in darkness. Employers differ the accommodations they offer workers, so seek one that provides access to food, water, shelter from the elements, and bathroom facilities. Farm workers must take precautions to avoid both sunburn and sunstroke. In early spring or autumn, cold, wind, and rain can also be factors in your day.

As noted above, the work of farm workers changes with the growing cycle of the crop. Harvesting is usually the busiest time, when you may be asked to put in extra hours to be sure all of the crop is picked and packed for shipping at the appropriate point of ripeness. Harvesting of delicate fruits is still done by hand, but certain crops are harvested by machines. You might be taught how to drive a tractor and how to use farm equipment like a combine or thresher, skills that can be essential to your future advancement. Most likely you will work on a crew that will function like an assembly line, with each worker having a specific function in the process of picking, packing, and loading the produce in the field. As you gain experience and demonstrate responsibility, you may get to move up to be a driver or crew leader.

Who You'll Work For

- ✳ Farm labor contractors
- ✳ Large, agribusiness companies
- ✳ Small farms
- ✳ Orchards
- ✳ Vineyards

Where You'll Work

Farm work is seasonal, with planting and harvesting the busiest times of year. The work is, obviously, mostly outdoors in fields, orchards, or vineyards. Long hours and six- or seven-day workweeks are common during planting and harvesting seasons. Farm workers are outside for many hours in all kinds of weather. The sun can be especially hard to deal with, but there also may be cold, wind, and rain. Working during all of the daylight hours may mean commuting to and from work in the dark. During the workday, there may be limited access to water, food, shelter, and bathroom facilities.

Since farm work is seasonal, you may need to obtain alternative employment in the off-season. Some farm workers, called migrant workers, move to new locations as crops ripen or to begin a growing

Let's Talk Trends

Agricultural jobs in general are expected to decline for the foreseeable future, but job turnover is high and opportunities should prove readily available for the foreseeable future. Consolidation of farms, technical advances in farm equipment, and trade agreements with foreign countries are mainly responsible for the projected decline in overall jobs. Farm workers are increasingly likely to be employed by farm labor contractors rather than being directly hired by the farms themselves.

season. This unsettled lifestyle is sometimes temporarily enjoyable to younger workers. Some jobs come with bunk-style shared housing but some jobs do not provide accommodation. It depends, in part, on the size of the agricultural operation and the distance to suitable housing for the workers.

The Inside Scoop: Q&A

Deb Sullivan
Farmer
Litchfield, Maine

Q: *How did you get your job?*

A: I grew up in the middle of a large city. I hated it. I always wanted horses and cows. When I was young, my parents, brother, and I would go out to buy sweet corn every summer Sunday after church at a local dairy farm. The first place I went was to the barn to play with the calves and pat the cows. Later on the nephew of the farmers became a veterinarian and raised racing quarter horses. I got to visit both the horses and the cows! I was in heaven.

I got a job when I turned sixteen and saved enough money to buy my first horse, which I supported. I became an apprentice horse trainer and learned horse breeding and raising. . . . I met my husband to be when I boarded my horses at his stable. He had the same dream . . . a dairy farm. Since dairying was almost impossible to get into in Massachusetts at the time, we moved to Maine with our two young sons. We finally got our dairy farm. I had a herd of dairy goats as well as dairy cattle and did well with milk production from both animals.

We set up the cattle milk machines to accommodate the goats and mixed the goat milk in with the cows' milk. We started getting a premium price for it because the protein and butter fat went up and the bacteria count went down. Only our sales rep knew we had the goats' milk piped in with the cows.

I still have horses and goats. My horses are used mostly as

(Continued on next page)

(continued from previous page)

pasture pets these days, but I still raise the goats. I have four dairy goats left from the original herd, but I have since added Boer goats to the mix. Boer goats are meat goats, and goat meat, or *chevon*, is becoming popular due to its low fat–low cholesterol content. I still milk the dairy goats but, instead of selling the milk, I make cheese, soap, butter, pudding, custard, and lotions from what milk I don't use in the house for drinking. I sell the male kids for meat, and a very select group of buck kids for breeding. The doe kids are either kept as replacements or sold for breeding. I have a full time job to support my livestock hobby, but the kid and soap sales help pay the feed bill. I am a small farm now, but still run it like I did the big farm years ago.

Q: *What do you like best about your job?*

A: I feel at peace when I am with my animals. I have rheumatoid arthritis, so the work keeps my joints limber. I get a real good feeling when an animal I have bred wins at shows or produces a record amount of milk. After being at work all day, the down time I have with my animals is a great stress reliever.

Q: *What's the most challenging part of your job?*

A: As with any type of farming, making a living is the biggest challenge. Milk and livestock prices are very low, while the price of feed, fuel, supplies, veterinary care . . . the normal day-to-day business costs . . . continue to rise. Only farms that have been in the family and are paid off can make a living.

Q: *What are the keys to success to being a farm worker?*

A: Four keys to success . . . hard work, long hours is the biggest key. Getting higher education at an agricultural college will help the business end as well as the animal husbandry part. Being able to run the farm as a business while still realizing that you are dealing with live animals is a major issue. You must learn to think with your brain and not let your heart rule the business. I had a hard time with culling. I still do. I get attached to my animals. . . . Some of them end up being shipped to slaughter; it's a fact of life. If you can't deal with it, then farming may not be for you.

Your Typical Day

Here are the highlights for a typical day for a farm worker on a large agribusiness farm during harvest season.

✔ **Get up before dawn.** Because most agricultural work is performed outdoors, laborers rely on natural light to see what they are doing. In order to take advantage of all the daylight in the fields, it is necessary to travel to work while it is still dark.

✔ **Fill containers with produce.** Containers that are appropriate for whatever fruit or vegetable you are picking will be provided at the end of every row in the field. It may be part of your job to load the empty containers onto a truck and drive them to the field, or you and the other workers may ride on the truck with the containers out to the place where you stopped picking the previous day.

✔ **Load containers for transport.** When darkness falls, you will be forced by lack of light to leave the fields and pack up the produce that you have picked so it can be shipped to packaging and distribution centers. This part of your job may involve heavy lifting or—increasingly as technology advances and farming becomes more automated—it may involve operating equipment that packs and stacks produce for transport.

What You Can Do Now

✴ Look up information on agriculture-related careers on the Internet or at your local library. There are some careers that you might find more lucrative or appealing than that of farm worker but they may require education beyond the high school level.

✴ Look for summer jobs as a farm worker. The job does not require a high school degree so there is nothing stopping you getting a job during summer vacation while you are still in school.

✴ Begin studying Spanish, if you do not already speak it.

What Training You'll Need

No previous education or training is needed to obtain a job as a farm worker. It is one of the least-skilled jobs available, which is one reason it appeals to immigrants, both legal and illegal, who lack English language skills and, in some cases, lack any formal education. All of the training you will need can be obtained on the job. This includes any equipment that you may have to operate. There isn't really any place to learn to use farm equipment except on a farm!

How to Talk Like a Pro

Here are a few terms of the trade:

- ✴ **Combine** A machine, either self-propelled or drawn by a tractor, that cuts, threshes, and cleans a standing crop such as grains or beans.
- ✴ **Crop rotation** The practice of growing different crops on the same land from year to year to help preserve the nutrients in the soil.
- ✴ **Power take-off (PTO)** A shaft on the rear of a tractor that is driven by the tractor's motor. It supplies rotative power to attachments such as balers, mowers, and combines.

How to Find a Job

The best part of being a farm laborer is the ease of finding employment. During planting and harvest season, there are usually plenty of jobs, and farmers and agribusinesses often complain that they have more work than workers. Since most farm workers do not speak English, look for advertisements for farm laborers in Spanish-language publications. You can ask farms if they are hiring directly, but the trend now is for workers to be employed by farm labor contractors. These contractors will provide workers to different farms on an as-needed basis.

Secrets for Success

See the suggestions below and turn to the appendix for advice on résumés and interviews.

- ✴ Love your work. What you don't get in salary and benefits or upward mobility you need to find in satisfaction in working with your hands on the land, growing the food we eat.
- ✴ Follow directions and be prompt and responsible.

Reality Check

Farm work is a low-paid profession. The work is often physically demanding, subject to the vagaries of weather, and only seasonally available. Increased mechanization is reducing the number of available jobs. There is an appeal to working outdoors, on the land, but think seriously about the trade-offs involved in salary, work environment, and stability.

Some Other Jobs to Think About

★ Grounds maintenance worker. These laborers look after the landscaping in a variety of settings. The work is not highly skilled, or highly paid, but it varies seasonally and you could work at college campuses, golf courses, sports facilities, corporate office complexes, malls, schools, parks, private homes, and anyplace else with landscaping that must be trimmed, planted, watered, and otherwise maintained. (See Chapter 1 for more information.)

★ Nursery or greenhouse worker. Employees of a commercial nursery grow plants that will be purchased and transplanted. They care for seedlings, prune and fertilize young plants, and advise customers on which plants to choose for their growing environment. (See Chapter 3 for more information.)

★ Livestock laborer. A livestock laborer is a similar type of agricultural worker, but instead of caring for crops you would be caring for chickens, cattle, pigs, or other animals that are raised for human consumption. (See Chapter 6 for more information.)

How You Can Move Up

★ If you prove yourself to be a competent and reliable worker, and if you have good communication skills, you might advance to a supervisory position such as crew leader. It will be an asset if you can speak Spanish.

★ To move beyond the level of laborer or labor supervisor, you are likely to need a degree in agricultural science or farm management. With such a degree in hand, you could become a farm manager.

✮ Related jobs that you could aspire to include professions such as purchasing agents for farms or farm-products companies, or you might become a farmer yourself.

Web Sites to Surf

National FFA Organization. This site provides information about education and jobs in the agricultural sciences.   http://www.ffa.org

National Farmworker Jobs Program. Site run by the U.S. Department of Labor that provides information to help unemployed and underemployed farm workers achieve economic self-sufficiency.   http://www.doleta.gov/msfw

U.S. Department of Agriculture. The USDA Web site provides general information about agricultural developments, regulations and employment. http://www.usda.gov/wps/portal/usdahome

Be outstanding in your field

Livestock Laborer

Make working with live animals your living

Nurture the next generation of food

Livestock Laborer

Have you eaten a hamburger recently? How about a turkey sandwich or a piece of fried chicken? Before that beef or poultry ended up on your plate, it was an animal that was bred for food, probably raised on a diet designed to bulk it up quickly, slaughtered, then processed and packaged and shipped to the local store or restaurant where you bought it. It's a long way from a steer grazing in a field to a ground sirloin patty sizzling on your grill. Someone has to care for animals that are raised for food. The job of a livestock laborer is hard, but many jobs are available in this traditional field.

Is This Job for You?

To find out if being a livestock laborer is a good fit for you, read each of the following statements and answer "Yes" or "No."

Yes No **1.** Can you tolerate being around animals that are being raised for meat?

Yes No **2.** Do you not mind getting wet and dirty on the job?

Yes No **3.** Are you willing to do physical labor all day for your work?

Yes No **4.** Do you accept that the farm animals you work with sometimes may be difficult to manage?

Yes No **5.** Can you tolerate concentrated smells of animal excrement?

Yes No **6.** Can you tolerate being on your feet all day and doing some heavy lifting?

Yes No **7.** Can you exercise caution in the use of hazardous machinery and equipment?

Yes No **8.** Are you capable of participating in animal-management activities such as branding, castrating, and debeaking?

Yes No **9.** Can you listen to and follow directions?

Yes No **10.** Do you have good coordination and balance?

If you can answer "Yes" to most of these questions, read on to find out more about a career in the livestock industry.

Let's Talk Money

The average hourly rate for livestock laborers in 2004 was $8.31 per hour. Livestock laborers are rarely unionized, and the jobs tend to lack benefits.

What You'll Do

A livestock laborer's work depends upon the type of animals that are being raised. Animals commonly raised for food include poultry, cattle, sheep, pigs, and fish. There are even bee farms that produce honey. As you can imagine, the work you'd perform on a fish farm is considerably different from what you'd do on a cattle ranch.

Even with the same type of animal, the work varies by the purpose for which they are being raised. Cattle, for example, are raised for beef and also for veal and milk. Cattle raised for beef are kept in feedlots or in pastures where they graze. Out West, they often graze on rangeland instead of in fenced pastures. Usually, if they are grass-fed at all, it is not for their entire lives. Most spend some time before slaughter fattening up in feedlots, where they are fed crops that are grown for this purpose. The care of beef cattle resembles the classic cowboy image, except that technology has changed how most of the work is performed. Instead of riding on horseback to patrol the fence line and make any necessary repairs, today you would be driving a truck loaded with equipment for repairs and maintenance. You still have to herd the cattle, driving them from one pasture to another as seasons change and grass gets depleted, but, again, you are likely to do this with GPS (Global Positioning System)-equipped vehicles—including helicopters—rather than on horseback, and getting cattle to move where you want them to go is more likely to involve an electric cattle prod than a herding dog. The steak-bound calves are still castrated, branded, vaccinated, and given antibiotics and other drugs, but the process is highly mechanized now. The work is still performed outdoors in all weather, and it is still seasonal, but it is less labor-intensive than of old.

Now let's contrast that work environment with a dairy farm. Dairy cows must be milked twice a day. This process is also highly mechanized today, with milking parlors that feature milking machines to which you hook up the cow's udder and it does the milking for you. But the cows still need to be brought in from their pasture twice a day, and there is a seasonal cycle of breeding, pregnancy, and calving on the farm. Cows and calves often get sick and need special care, and the milking parlor and equipment must be thoroughly cleaned and disinfected after each milking. The work is repetitive and time-consuming. It also takes place outdoors in all weather, and is seasonal in nature, but there is an indoor component of it due to the milking parlor.

Poultry and egg farms tend to be the quintessential "factory farms" where chickens are debeaked and given antibiotics so they can live packed into tiny cages without harming one another from the stress or succumbing to infections. Sometimes hundreds of thousands of chickens are packed into one building. The work here involves feeding and cleaning, but the cages are arranged in such a way that even this process is highly mechanized. On most large egg farms, eggs tumble down a chute onto a conveyor belt where they are now cleaned, sorted, and packaged by machine, not by workers.

However, the fastest-growing segment of the food market is for organic products—especially milk and eggs. The systems of production for these products often include a concern for animal welfare. Because their produce would lose its premium price if they were administered the various drugs given to most farm animals, creatures in the organic chain must be treated well so they don't become diseased. Companies in the organics marketplace vary in how they treat their workers, but many put a similar value on worker conditions as on the animals'.

The work in aquaculture (fish farms) is quite different from the type of labor involved in raising land animals. You might be stocking ponds, feeding fish stocks, and managing nets and water filtration systems, as well as harvesting and packaging fish and other aquatic life.

Let's Talk Trends

Overall employment in the agricultural sector is projected to decline as mechanization enables factory farms to get by with fewer workers. This trend is offset by the fact that job turnover is high. Also, the re-emergence of traditional farmers who sell through either green markets or organic companies presents a growing, if still small, niche for farm worker employment outside the dominant, intensive model.

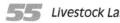

Who You'll Work For

- ✴ Factory farms raising poultry, cattle, or pigs
- ✴ Egg and poultry farms
- ✴ Pig farms
- ✴ Beef cattle ranches
- ✴ Dairy farms
- ✴ Fish farms (aquaculture)
- ✴ Apiaries (bee farms)

The Inside Scoop: Q&A

Danielle Brison
Livestock laborer
Bremen, Ohio

Q: *How did you get your job?*

A: I acquired my job while in FFA (Future Farmers of America). The client called in, and it was assigned to me. FFA is a very educational program if you are wanting to work in the farm industry.

Q: *What do you like best about your job?*

A: What I liked best about my job was feeding the calves their milk out of bottles in the morning and afternoon. They solely depend on you; I would say that they think of you as their mother.

Q: *What's the most challenging part of your job?*

A: The most challenging part of my job was getting up at 3:30 in the morning and it is continuous repetition.

Q: *What are the keys to success to being a livestock laborer?*

A: I would say that the most important keys to success in this industry are loving what you do and truly caring about your animals. It takes a lot of drive and motivation to get up early every day and do the same thing over and over again.

Where You'll Work

If you work with large animals like cattle, you are likely to spend most if not all of your time outdoors. Beef cattle ranches tend to be found in the Southwest and West. Feedlots tend to be more numerous in the Plains states. Dairy farms, which involve some indoor work in the milking parlor, are concentrated in the East and Midwest but can be found almost everywhere. Hog farms are found all over but are more numerous in the Southeast and the Plains states. Poultry and egg farms are fairly evenly distributed around the country, as are apiaries. Aquaculture is concentrated near the coasts, particularly the Pacific Northwest. Wherever you live, some type of animal is raised for food near you.

Agricultural workers tend to work longer hours than workers in other fields. Animals need to be fed and cared for seven days a week, including holidays. This may mean that you work in shifts. Unlike crops, animals need care year round, but the work is still seasonal in nature. Spring is a busy time with calving and lambing. There are also particular times of year when castrating, branding, vaccinating, and slaughtering take place.

Your Typical Day

Here are the highlights for a typical day for a livestock laborer on a dairy farm.

✔ **Bring cows into milking parlor.** Cows are creatures of habit and they are usually lined up at the gate at the proper time. There will be a series of chutes directing them into a line for the milking machines. The rows are raised so that you do not need to bend over to hook the udders up to the machines.

✔ **Clean milking parlor.** Strict regulations govern the sanitation of milking parlors. You will need to thoroughly spray and scrub the facility after each use. You will also need to clean the milk tanks after they are emptied into trucks and monitor the temperature and bacterial contamination in the tanks. You will also track milk production per cow so that low-producing cows can be culled and the offspring of particularly high-producing cows can be kept to strengthen the herd.

✔ **Bring cows in again.** Yep, just as you did in the morning. The cows need to be milked twice a day, so the whole cycle repeats.

What You Can Do Now

✯ If you live in a rural area, join the local 4-H club and take agricultural science classes at your high school. If you live in the city, these courses and clubs might not be as accessible to you, but see if there is anything within commuting distance.

✯ Learn all you can about the livestock industry. Read and watch videos about life on various types of farms. Visit local farms, if you can. This will help you decide which animal and lifestyle is right for you.

✯ Look for summer jobs on local farms. Since there are no educational requirements for this work, you can get a job while you are still in school. There are certain laws restricting work that is considered dangerous to those over 18, but some jobs will be open to you.

What Training You'll Need

Most agricultural workers, including livestock laborers, do not have a high school diploma. The lack of formal qualifications or experience for the job attracts immigrants, both legal and illegal, who lack English language skills. Most jobs offer on-the-job training. The more factory-like and mechanized the work, the less a potential employer is going to care about skills or experience. The one sector of the industry where experience may be a factor is beef cattle ranching. A ranch manager is likely to favor applicants who have had some experience handling cattle. Also, some high-end and smaller farms may look for applicants who have taken agricultural science classes. This is particularly true on breeding farms.

How to Talk Like a Pro

Here are a few terms of the trade:

✯ **Steer** Castrated bull calf, usually raised for beef.

✯ **Animal unit (AU)** A unit for measuring feed consumption and animal density on farms. One animal unit is usually equivalent to 1,000 pounds or about one mature cow.

✯ **Freshen** A fresh cow has just given birth and is beginning a lactation cycle.

How to Find a Job

To find a job, approach farms in your area and ask if they are hiring. Advertisements for jobs might appear in local papers. Look at Spanish-language publications as many livestock laborers are native Spanish speakers. There are some independent recruiters who fill job openings for large operations such as factory poultry farms. If there is one in your area, register with them and they will alert you to job openings. There are some online job sites that list agricultural jobs but most jobs advertised online are likely to be higher-level managerial or inspection/compliance-related jobs that require special training, certification, or experience. Your best bet is to ask directly at local farms. There is a high turnover rate in agricultural jobs, so there are frequently entry-level openings. Keep checking at the same farms even if when you have checked before there have been no vacancies. You have a better chance of getting hired if you are flexible about your hours and exhibit a willingness to work less desirable shifts.

Secrets for Success

See the suggestions below and turn to the appendix for advice on résumés and interviews.

⚝ Have a high tolerance for routine. Animals, as living creatures with minds of their own, can be unpredictable. This will provide some variety in your workday. Yet, the overriding characteristic of life on a factory farm is the routine. The animals are kept on a strict schedule, designed to maximize productivity, and this means repetition for the workers who care for them.

⚝ Stay focused while working; with big animals and heavy equipment, small mistakes can prove costly!

Reality Check

As related already, the cowboy is a bygone figure of the American landscape. Livestock laborers are in the business of food production, and in this industry animals are seen as economic units of production.

Some Other Jobs to Think About

✴ Animal caretaker. Animal caretakers work in shelters that house unwanted or stray animals. They keep records, feed, clean cages, test animals for temperament, obtain veterinary care for sick or injured animals, and assist in euthanizing unwanted animals. They also may deal directly with the public, facilitating adoptions and screening potential adopters. Animal caretakers also work in boarding kennels and doggy daycare facilities.

✴ Groom. Grooms care for riding and driving horses in stables. They feed their charges, cool them off and rub them down after exercise, bathe them, and make them look presentable for shows or other appearances. They also care for all of the tack (equipment, such as saddles and harnesses) that the horse uses. Of course, they also clean stalls!

✴ Butcher, slaughterer, or meatpacker. Butchers and related occupations are the next step in the process of turning the steer that the livestock laborer raises into hamburger for your table. Animals are shipped from farms to slaughterhouses where they are killed, chopped up, and packaged. (See Chapter 8 for more information.)

How You Can Move Up

✴ If you prove yourself to be a competent and reliable worker, you may move up to a supervisory role.

✴ If you would like to become a farm manager or a specialist in an area such as breeding or inspecting livestock, you will need to pursue further education and training. See if a local college offers an associate's or bachelor's degree in agricultural science. In most degree programs, you can specialize in a certain area such as breeding or inspection. The FFA Web site provides useful information about educational options. Ask your employer what additional education you would need to move up to a position that interests you.

Web Sites to Surf

National FFA Organization. This site provides information about education and jobs in the agricultural sciences.   http://www.ffa.org

National Farmworker Jobs Program. Site run by the U.S. Department of Labor that provides information to help unemployed and underemployed Farm Workers achieve economic self-sufficiency.   http://www.doleta.gov/msfw

U.S. Department of Agriculture. The USDA Web site provides general information about agricultural developments, regulations and employment. http://www.usda.gov/wps/portal/usdahome

Work with common and exotic animals

Pest Control Technician/ Animal Control Officer

Rescue abused and neglected animals

Rid houses of uninvited pests

Pest Control Technician/Animal Control Officer

This chapter covers two jobs that are actually quite different. They are featured together because they both involve the issue of humans and animals living side by side in the modern world. Wild animals and insects sometimes settle in people's houses and cause problems, ranging from just a nuisance to serious health and structural issues. Pest control technicians eradicate insects, vermin, and wild animals that have taken up residence in buildings. Domestic animals like cats and dogs sometimes escape or are abandoned by their owners and need to be taken off the streets so that they do not get hurt or killed, and so they do not pose a threat to people and other animals. Unfortunately, pets are also sometimes abused or neglected by their owners and need to be rescued from a bad situation. Animal control officers (ACOs) handle this important job.

Is This Job for You?

To find out if being a pest control technician or animal control officer is a good fit for you, read each of the following statements and answer "Yes" or "No."

Yes	*No*	**1.**	Do you love animals and hate to see them abused or neglected?
Yes	*No*	**2.**	Can you accept the risks associated with working with strange animals that might be frightened, injured, or unsocialized?
Yes	*No*	**3.**	Can you deal with people who may be hostile?
Yes	*No*	**4.**	Does educating people about proper care for their animals appeal to you?
Yes	*No*	**5.**	Are you observant and detail-oriented?
Yes	*No*	**6.**	Can prepare reports and take photographs that may be used in prosecution of cases of cruelty and neglect?
Yes	*No*	**7.**	Are you prepared to crawl into basements, attics, and other dirty and inaccessible spaces as a regular part of your job?
Yes	*No*	**8.**	Could you manage any phobias you might have of insects, rodents, or snakes?

Yes   No   **9.**   Would you enjoy educating people about ways to keep their homes free of pests?

Yes   No   **10.**   Can you use the necessary care to work with pesticides and other chemicals on a regular basis?

If you can answer "Yes" to most of these questions, read on to find out more about a career in the fields of pest management or animal control.

What You'll Do

An ACO enforces city and state animal welfare laws. She or he investigates reported cases of animal cruelty or neglect and has the authority to impound animals, issue citations, and make arrests. Conducting inspections and issuing permits is also part the of the ACO's responsibilities. There is a lot of paperwork involved in this job. An ACO must keep accurate records and prepare reports on all cases, including taking photographs of neglected and abused animals and the conditions in which they were living. The successful prosecution of animal abusers depends upon how well the ACO document the cases.

Education is also part of an ACO's duties. When an ACO investigates cases of neglect, instead of arresting the offender sometimes the ACO will issue a warning and educate the person about proper care for animals. The ACO will then make follow-up visits to ensure compliance. This strategy can be effective for offenders who are not being deliberately cruel or neglectful but who are genuinely ignorant of their animals' needs.

Let's Talk Money

The salaries of ACOs vary by location. In larger, wealthier municipalities, the salary paid by the city is going to be higher than the salaries paid by counties in poorer and more rural areas. The current starting salary paid by the city of Los Angeles, for example, is $2,815 per month. This should be construed as the higher end of the possible pay range.

Median hourly wages for pest control technicians were $12.71 in 2004. The salary range varied from less than $8.13 to more than $20.19 per hour.

A pest control technician will travel to buildings and nearby areas that are infested with some type of pest and attempt to eradicate it. In some cases, the pest control technician may have to identify the species of pest and find creative ways of repelling pests when conventional techniques fail. Gaining access to areas that pests inhabit may be challenging. Climbing, crawling, and squeezing into small spaces are a regular feature of the job.

Once the pest has been located and identified, the pest control technician has a variety of methods to eliminate it. In some cases, chemical pesticides are used. Due to their certification, pest control technicians have access to regulated chemicals that are restricted from use by the general public. The safe use of these chemicals requires equipment, including respirators, that can be heavy and hot to wear. But pesticides are not the only option for eradicating pests. The use of a combination of pest control techniques, called Integrated Pest Management (IPM), is increasingly popular and considered safer and more effective than the use of pesticides alone.

Who You'll Work For

* ⭐ City law enforcement agencies
* ⭐ Counties
* ⭐ Privately run humane societies with local government contracts
* ⭐ Pest management companies

Let's Talk Trends

Animal control is a stressful and demanding job, but it is a career that inspires dedication, so turnover is not as high as in other high-stress animal care occupations, such as shelter work. As pet ownership increases, job opportunities are likely to increase in this and related fields.

Job prospects are likely to be very good for pest control technicians for several reasons. The occupation is generally considered unappealing, which means that demand for workers is usually higher than supply. The job—unlike that of ACO—has a high turnover rate, leading to continual job openings. Also, as the population becomes more affluent and the standard of living increases, demand will be higher for professional pest control. The population is also shifting towards the Sunbelt, the area of the country most prone to pests.

Where You'll Work

As an animal control officer, your job environment will depend upon whether you are based in an urban or rural area. In an urban area, you will be driving an official law enforcement vehicle, and your day will consist of driving around to houses and apartment complexes to investigate complaints and conduct follow-up visits to ensure compliance. You may have to go into dangerous neighborhoods to pursue cases of cruelty and neglect as well as investigate dog- or cockfighting rings. You will have to do a lot of driving to follow up on reports of stray dogs, wildlife coming into urban areas, or rabid animals. In rural areas, your calls are more likely to involve larger animals such as horses, and you may have to drive longer distances to get out to farms. You will also spend part of your time at animal shelters, where you will drop off animals that you are being impounded, photograph them, and follow-up on their progress. You may use this information when you are called to present evidence in court, another important facet of your job.

A pest control technician works for a company that responds to calls from clients, members of the public with an animal-related problem. As a technician, you are likely to spend much of your time in your company's truck or van, driving to job sites. Depending on the population density of your area, you may be called mainly to houses or primarily to apartment or commercial buildings. The types of pests that you will confront will also vary considerably by geographic location. One type of pest that is making a resurgence everywhere is bed bugs. You are likely to encounter them wherever you work.

Your Typical Day

Here are the highlights for a typical day for an animal control officer employed by a medium-sized city.

✔ **Follow up on previous calls.** If you have no urgent new calls, you may begin your workday by driving around to see if owners who have been ordered to take better care of their pets are doing so. You will check for adequate food, water and shelter, a safe environment free of hazards, and assess the overall condition of the animals. You must record everything that you see. If you discover noncompliance, you may end up impounding animals from the site.

✔ **Attend to the day's schedule of calls.** When someone phones in animal control to report a suspected case of abuse or a stray animal in the area, you will get a call on your radio with an address to go to. If there are more calls than you can cover in one day, you may start each workday with a list of calls to make as you can get to them.

✔ **Accurately and thoroughly record your findings for the day.** Keeping accurate records is an important part of your job. It could mean the difference between an animal dying or being rescued, and successful prosecution of abuse cases depends upon detailed written and photographical evidence.

What You Can Do Now

⚡ Applicants for animal control vacancies are usually required to demonstrate at least a year of experience in animal care. Look for a summer job assisting in a shelter, grooming salon, boarding kennel, or veterinarian's office. Most of these places hire high school students to clean kennels and assist with other menial tasks. This experience could mean the difference between getting a job or not being chosen.

⚡ If you aspire to be a pest control technician, it will be to your benefit to take chemistry and math classes in high school.

⚡ Both of these jobs require considerable driving, and applicants without a clean driving record are usually automatically disqualified from consideration. Make sure your driving record is clean and stays clean.

What Training You'll Need

Since animal control is a branch of law enforcement, applicants have to face many of the same hurdles as police academy recruits. There is usually a physical abilities test that assesses flexibility, agility, and physical strength. A medical examination is often required, and this will include a psychological screening—including a personality inventory evaluation. A comprehensive background check is required, along with a written test. These usually must be successfully passed before the candidate moves on to other areas of screening. New recruits undergo a lengthy probationary period of on-the-job training where they accompany an experienced ACO on calls. Many of these

The Inside Scoop: Q&A

Richard McGoldrick
Animal control officer
Denmark, Maine

Q: *How did you get your job?*

A: I was retired after selling my business. My wife, Marilyn, and I raised dogs and I had been brought up with horses. The local chief of police asked me if I would help out with animal control. I got certified and became an animal control officer (ACO). Soon I was doing the same in nine other towns, so I was covering ten towns in western Maine.

Q: *What do you like best about your job?*

A: The thing I like best about this work is that each day I have a score or report card that allows me to honestly know and feel good about the fact that I have done something to improve the existence of at least one or maybe several animals. Most of the times the animals involved are dogs, cats, horses, and sometimes other types of farm animals. The way we help is to make sure all the animals in our area are kept and cared for as the law requires. It is very satisfying to cause an improvement in the environmental conditions of the animals and also to help educate the owners or keepers as to how they can do better. It is also satisfying to charge the owners or keepers that continuously ignore the requirements and show beyond a doubt that they do not care about the law and even worse about their animals.

Q: *What's the most challenging part of your job?*

A: The most challenging part is to make sure to stay in touch with all methods of handling all the types of animals. You must keep yourself and your staff educated and up to date on animal handling. This is for the safety of the handlers and the animals. An equally challenging facet of the job is to control your emotions, actions and attitudes towards the people involved in animal cases. Sometimes the first things that are evident as you arrive on a scene are enough to possibly make it very difficult to investigate

(Continued on next page)

(continued from previous page)

thoroughly and effectively! Handle all with respect, politeness, and fairness, and show a professional knowledge.

Q: *What are the keys to success to being an animal control officer?*

A: The key to success in animal control is to approach every thing from the point of view of the animal! You are the *only* voice that animal has! If you can do this you will feel as I do: Why haven't I done this all my life!

requirements are waived in rural or less affluent areas that have a part-time ACO.

The training and certification required to become a pest control technician is extensive, but the good news is that you can complete much of it on the job—often at your employer's expense. As a new hire, you will be classified as an apprentice technician. You will have to complete general training in safe pesticide handling and use before you will be allowed to perform any pest control services for clients. In addition to the general training, you will need to attend training in specific types of pest control, such as termite abatement, rodent control, and fumigation. Training requirements vary by state but usually involve at least 60 hours on the job and 10 hours of specific training for each category. Once apprentices have completed this basic training, they can assist licensed applicators in performing pest control services under supervision. After obtaining additional education and experience, apprentices can take an examination to become certified applicators. Most states require that applicators attend continuing education and take additional examinations to be re-certified at intervals of one or more years.

How to Talk Like a Pro

Here are a few terms of the trade:

★ **Integrated pest management (IPM)** An increasingly popular method of pest control that relies on safer and more environmentally friendly means than pesticides, including natural predators, pest-resistant plants, and other non-chemical methods of discouraging pest infestation.

✴ **Catch pole** Main tool used by ACOs to catch frightened or unsocialized animals. It consists of a metal pole with a noose on the end. When the noose is placed around the animal's neck, the ACO can tighten it via a lever on the pole. It keeps the animal at arm's length to reduce the risk of injury to the handler.

✴ **Fumigation** A technique for eliminating pests, usually insects, that involves sealing all openings to an area and pumping pesticides into the sealed space. The chemicals used are usually highly toxic so fumigation must be conducted in a conscientious manner, with careful control over when it is safe for humans and pets to re-enter the area.

How to Find a Job

Since animal control officers are local government employees, you need to check for openings wherever your city or town advertises civil service job vacancies. If you are unsure where to look, call the mayor's office; they should be able to direct you to the correct Web site. You may find listings in your local paper, but some municipalities are advertising vacancies exclusively online now. If you live in a rural area, you are more likely to be hired by the county. Look under services in your local telephone book and call the animal control office. They should be able to tell you everything you need to know about finding and applying for vacancies.

Potential pest control technicians can phone local pest control companies directly and ask if they are hiring. Vacancies may also be advertised in local classified job listings.

Secrets for Success

See the suggestions below and turn to the appendix for advice on résumés and interviews.

✴ Love, really love, animals. Animal control work is inappropriate for you if you are indifferent to the suffering of the animals whose welfare you are assigned to protect.

✴ Never cut corners with safety and stay up to date on newer, less toxic, pest management techniques.

Reality Check

Both animal control and pest management involve job-specific risks. Workers in both professions are at risk from bites and scratches from frightened or rabid animals. Animal control officers face an additional danger from the owners, who often do not take kindly to their animals being impounded or to being told how to take care of them. Pest control technicians are exposed to dangerous chemicals on an ongoing basis, which poses a health risk that only you can decide if you are willing to bear.

Some Other Jobs to Think About

* Animal caretaker. Animal caretakers work in shelters that house unwanted or stray animals. They keep records, feed, clean cages, test animals for temperament, obtain veterinary care for sick or injured animals, and assist in euthanizing unwanted animals. They may also deal directly with the public, facilitating adoptions and screening potential adopters. Animal caretakers also work in boarding kennels and doggy daycare facilities.

* Animal trainer. Like animal control officers, animal trainers are involved in teaching pet owners how to properly care for and handle their pets. Trainers often get to work one-on-one with owners and their pets for an extended period and have the satisfaction of seeing progress in overcoming behavioral problems. The increasing popularity of pets has led to recent growth in this gratifying but not very lucrative field.

* Building inspector. Building inspectors assess houses and other structures for soundness and safety before they are sold to new owners. Searching for signs of infestation by termites and other pests is one of the main items on a building inspector's checklist.

How You Can Move Up

* With additional certifications, training, and experience, animal control officers sometimes can move up to a supervisory role. Upward mobility is dependent upon the size of the jurisdiction. A county with just one ACO cannot really offer a higher-level position. On the other hand, a large municipality is likely to have a hierarchy of animal control staff, with supervisors overseeing other ACOs.

✴ The pest control industry changes quickly and just to maintain your job, never mind moving up, pest control technicians need to attend continuing education classes and take periodic examinations to renew and enhance their certifications. One you have several years experience as a licensed pesticide applicator, you can sit exams to become a supervisor. These examinations are administered by states, and requirements vary among states.

Web Sites to Surf

National Animal Control Association. This site contains information about the training and certification you need to become an animal control officer. It also includes information on jobs and earnings.   http://www.nacanet.org

National Pest Management Association, Inc. This is the national trade organization for the pest control industry.   http://www.pestworld.org

Florida Pest Management Association, Inc. Each state has its own pest control association. This is just one example. Search on the Internet for the one in your state.   http://www.fpca.org

Practice one of the oldest human skills

Butcher/Various Meat-Processing Occupations

Put food on the table—for yourself and others!

Practice a trade you can apply anywhere

Butcher/Various Meat-Processing Occupations

If you have ever grilled a steak or cooked a Thanksgiving turkey, you have seen the handiwork of a butcher. Butchers take an animal, like a steer, and kill it, skin it, drain its blood, disembowel it, and cut it into the recognizable cuts of meat that you see in your local stores. The work of a butcher is not for everyone, but there are many related jobs in meat processing such as slaughterers, meat packers, and fish and poultry cutters. There are workers in processing plants engaged in all steps of the process from live animal to shrink-wrapped package.

Is This Job for You?

To find out if being a butcher is a good fit for you, read each of the following questions and answer "Yes" or "No."

Yes	No	**1.**	Can you tolerate an animal-processing environment?
Yes	No	**2.**	Are you comfortable killing animals for food?
Yes	No	**3.**	Do you have good eye-hand coordination?
Yes	No	**4.**	Can you learn to wield knives and other cutting implements skillfully and safely?
Yes	No	**5.**	Can you tolerate getting your clothes sloppy on a daily basis?
Yes	No	**6.**	Can you work all day on your feet and do some heavy lifting?
Yes	No	**7.**	Do you understand that meat-processing workers are more prone to injuries than most other workers?
Yes	No	**8.**	Can you work in the cold environment of a refrigerated room?
Yes	No	**9.**	Can you serve customers politely?
Yes	No	**10.**	Can you accurately weigh and label product for sale?

If you can answer "Yes" to most of these questions, read on to find out more about a career in the meat, poultry, and fish processing industries.

Let's Talk Money

Employees of the meat processing industry command wages that vary by skill, geographic region, and type of employer. Meat, poultry, and fish cutters in animal slaughtering and processing plants had the lowest earnings, with a median annual salary of $18,660 as of May 2004. Butchers and grocery store meat cutters earned an average salary of $27,030 in the same year. Some meat processing workers are unionized and receive benefits.

What You'll Do

Your work as a meat processor will depend on several factors. The first is the type of animal being cut up. Plants usually specialize in one type of animal, so if you work in a seafood processing plant you will disembowel, de-scale, and cut up fish, usually removing the head and fins. Some fish are further processed into steaks and fillets, and some are ground into fishmeal. Fish processing is often less removed from sales than other types of meat manufacturing so, as a fish cutter and trimmer (also called fish cleaner), you may dress fish as well as sell it directly to wholesale or retail customers.

Poultry cutters and trimmers work in an environment that is increasingly automated. Workers are usually stationed along a production line where they perform the same routine cutting task on each chicken or turkey that passes along the conveyor. Repetitive stress injuries are common in poultry processing facilities.

Cattle, pigs, sheep, and goats are usually cut into large wholesale slabs of meat at the slaughterhouses where they are killed. At a slaughterhouse, you might be involved in unloading animals destined for slaughter into holding pens, herding them into chutes for killing, stunning, and killing them, and then processing the carcass in various ways. Usually the head, limbs, tail, and organs are removed, and the animal is skinned and drained of blood before being cut up. The degree of further processing will depend upon the facility and its customers. Some plants produce cuts such as rounds, ribs, loins, and chunks. Others grind meat into hamburger and manufacture fabricated meat products such as luncheon meats and sausages.

The work of a butcher in a retail or wholesale establishment is different in that the butcher usually works with wholesale cuts of meat to precisely cut and trim them into steaks, chops, roasts, boneless cuts, and to fulfill specific customer requests.

Who You'll Work For

✴ Meat, poultry or fish processing plants

✴ Wholesalers

✴ Retail grocery stores

✴ Butcher shops

✴ Fish mongers

✴ Institutional food service facilities

✴ Slaughterhouses

Where You'll Work

Employees of a meat, poultry, or fish processing plant work in a factory-like atmosphere that is usually white and institutional-looking. The rooms are kept refrigerated to prevent the meat from spoiling, which may take some getting used to for new employees. Floors in slaughterhouses are usually slick with entrails, blood, and other bodily fluids, and the floors of refrigerated processing rooms are damp from condensation, blood, and fat. These conditions, combined with

Let's Talk Trends

Job turnover is relatively high in the meat processing industry due to low pay and poor working conditions, making it relatively easy to get a job. Employment prospects for lower-skilled workers in meat processing plants are expected to be better than for more highly skilled retail butchers. This is due to the consolidation of meat packaging and the trend toward making ready-to-heat, prepared meat products in manufacturing plants rather than having this work done at wholesalers and in stores.

cold temperatures and long hours of standing, lead to considerable risk of slip-and-fall accidents.

The presence and use of many cutting tools, including knives, cleavers, slicers, and power tools results in numerous cutting injuries to workers, including amputations. Although safety measures have been improved, workers in this industry still face considerable risk of serious and disabling injuries.

Butchers and fish cleaners in retail establishments often work in close spaces behind a sales counter. There is usually a refrigerated room for meat storage, and a variety of cutting and wrapping tools, but retail meat processing workers have a less repetitive job than plant workers.

Your Typical Day

Here are the highlights for a typical day for a poultry cutter in a poultry processing plant.

- ✔ **Punch in for shift and don hygienic clothing.** Most meat processing workers are required to wear hairnets, gloves, and some type of protective covering for their clothing and shoes.
- ✔ **Take up position on production line.** You will usually be assigned to a specific spot and task on the production line, performing the same cutting activity, such as clipping off the wings, on each bird that comes along a conveyor system.
- ✔ **Punch out after shift and go home.** When the whistle blows at the end of your shift, you'll punch out on the time clock and you will most likely head home, exhausted, for a much-needed shower and rest.

What You Can Do Now

- ✰ Look for an after-school or summer job apprenticing to a local butcher, working the deli or meat counter at your one of your neighborhood grocery stores, or, if you live near the coast, cleaning fish.
- ✰ Take a cooking class that teaches safe knife handling and use.
- ✰ Read up on the Web or at your local library about food-borne illnesses and health and safety regulations.

The Inside Scoop: Q&A

Fred Rosa
Butcher
Waltham, Massachusetts

Q: *How did you get your job?*

A: I work as a butcher in a family business in Guilford, Connecticut (Guilford Food Center). It is a small grocery store that specializes in fresh meats, deli, bakery and produce.

Q: *What do you like best about your job?*

A: Being part of a family business allows me to interact with the same clientele on a daily basis and build relationships while providing a community with fresh foods.

Q: *What's the most challenging part of your job?*

A: Coldness in the coolers and freezers. You definitely have to dress for the job, especially in the winter.

Q: *What are the keys to success to being a butcher?*

A: Being honest with your customers and always keeping the product fresh. Customers are smart and will be able to tell if it's not fresh, so to keep them coming back you have to make them happy every single day.

What Training You'll Need

There are no educational or training qualifications for most meat processing jobs. Most jobs in this field are considered to be very low-skilled occupations, and all the training that you need can be acquired on the job. The exception is the dying profession of butcher. Butchers are skilled in cutting meat to order and preparing specialized ready-to-cook meat products. They perform a greater variety of work than meat processing plant employees. In order to develop these skills, you need to apprentice with a butcher; however, as more meat processing is shifted from the retail sector to manufacturing facilities, the profession of butcher is becoming more of a craft than an everday trade. Opportunities may be limited compared with the past, but positions may still be found with gourmet vendors.

Health certification is required by some states for certain supervisory roles but it is usually not relevant to entry-level positions. Manual dexterity, and good eye-hand coordination are useful for working quickly with cutting tools; some sports and hobbies such as fishing may help in developing these skills.

How to Talk Like a Pro

Here are a few terms of the trade:

* **Wholesale cut** Portions of a quarter—such as round, loin, rib, chuck, flank, and brisket—that are sold to supermarkets where a butcher chops them into retail cuts.
* **Case-ready** Meat that is prepackaged at a processing plant so it can go directly into the display case in a grocery store.
* **Canner** Lowest USDA grade designation for beef; below cutter, standard, good, select, choice, and prime. Normally used in canned and ground meats and sausages.

How to Find a Job

Jobs in the meat processing industry are usually advertised locally. State employment agencies are one place to check for notices of vacancies, as is the classified section of your local newspaper. If you live in a geographic area with many Hispanic immigrants, you might try looking in Spanish-language publications as well. Also, there is no harm in going into local butcher shops and fish mongers, or to the meat section of your local grocery stores, and asking if they are hiring. Since quick, precise, and safe use of various cutting tools is the main component of the job, employers will look for manual dexterity and good eye-hand coordination in potential employees. It will also help if you present a tidy appearance to potential employers, with short, clean nails and your hair combed or tied back neatly.

Secrets for Success

See the following suggestions and turn to the appendix for advice on résumés and interviews.

✴ Have a strong stomach. There's just no other way to put it. Dealing with death, blood, gore, and their associated smells every day is not for someone with a delicate constitution.

✴ Always be mindful of what you are doing—your safety and other peoples' health depend on it.

Reality Check

The work can be hazardous and isn't always pretty. But you can draw satisfaction from knowing you are providing food for people to put on the table. Your pay may not be great, and some people may find what you do gory, but more than nine in ten North Americans regularly eat meat.

Some Other Jobs to Think About

✴ Food preparation worker. Food preparation workers assist chefs and cooks in restaurants, grocery stores, and caterers to prepare a large variety of foods to sell to the general public.

✴ Baker. Employees of commercial bakeries prepare baked goods for sale. Shift work is common and some bakers work overnight so that the baked goods are fresh for purchase in the morning.

✴ Fisher. Fishers work on boats to catch various types of seafood for human consumption. Some of the issues with cold and stress and smells are similar to those in the meat processing industry.

How You Can Move Up

✴ Advancement in the meat processing industry is usually based on experience. Those employed as butchers usually train under an experienced butcher for a year or two to learn skills involved in preparing specific cuts of meat, tying roasts, making sausage, and other specialized meat products. In some states, health certificates are required to prove that supervisory employees have had training in the safe handling of food to reduce the risk of contamination with food-borne pathogens.

✴ Employees of meat, poultry, and fish processing plants can move up to team leader and supervisory roles with sufficient experience and communication skills.

Web Sites to Surf

North American Meat Processors Association. A trade association for butchers and related meat processing occupations, NAMPA publishes an annual meat buyers' guide for butchers, a well-known reference for slicing and grading various cuts of meat.   http://www.namp.com/namp/default.asp

American Association of Meat Processors. This organization primarily represents employers, not employees, but its site has a lot of information about regulations and food safety.   http://www.aamp.com

Unlock your network

Appendix

Get your résumé ready

Ace your interview

Putting Your Best Foot Forward

When 20-year-old Justin Schulman started job-hunting for a position as a fitness trainer—the first step toward managing a fitness facility—he didn't mess around. "I immediately opened the Yellow Pages and started calling every number listed under health and fitness, inquiring about available positions," he recalls. Schulman's energy and enterprise paid off: He wound up with interviews that led to several offers of part-time work.

Schulman's experience highlights an essential lesson for job seekers: There are plenty of opportunities out there, but jobs won't come to you—especially the career-oriented, well-paying ones that that you'll want to stick with over time. You've got to seek them out.

Uncover Your Interests

Whether you're in high school or bringing home a full-time paycheck, the first step toward landing your ideal job is assessing your interests. You need to figure out what makes you tick. After all, there is a far greater chance that you'll enjoy and succeed in a career that taps into your passions, inclinations, and natural abilities. That's what happened with career-changer Scott Rolfe. He was already 26 when he realized he no longer wanted to work in the food industry. "I'm an avid outdoorsman," Rolfe says, "and I have an appreciation for natural resources that many people take for granted." Rolfe turned his passions into his ideal job as a forestry technician.

If you have a general idea of what your interests are, you're far ahead of the game. You may know that you're cut out for a health care career, for instance, or one in business. You can use a specific volume of Great Careers with a High School Diploma to discover what position to target. If you are unsure of your direction, check out the whole range of volumes to see the scope of jobs available.

You can also use interest inventories and skills-assessment programs to further pinpoint your ideal career. Your school or public librarian or guidance counselor should be able to help you locate such assessments. Web sites, such as America's Career InfoNet (http://www.acinet.org) and Jobweb.com, also offer interest inventories.

You'll find suggestions for Web sites related to specific careers at the end of each chapter in any Great Careers with a High School Diploma volume.

Unlock Your Network

The next stop toward landing the perfect job is networking. The word may make you cringe, but networking is simply introducing yourself and exchanging job-related and other information that may prove helpful to one or both of you. That's what Susan Tinker-Muller did. Quite a few years ago, she struck up a conversation with a fellow passenger on her commuter train. Little did she know that the natural interest she expressed in the woman's accounts payable department would lead to news about a job opening there. Tinker-Muller's networking landed her an entry-level position in accounts payable with MTV Networks. She is now the accounts payable administrator.

Tinker-Muller's experience illustrates why networking is so important. Fully 80 percent of openings are *never* advertised, and more than half of all employees land their jobs through networking, according to the U.S. Bureau of Labor Statistics. That's 8 out of 10 jobs that you'll miss if you don't get out there and talk with people. And don't think you can bypass face-to-face conversations by posting your résumé on job sites like Craigslist, Monster.com, and Hotjobs.com and then waiting for employers to contact you. That's so mid-1990s! Back then, tens of thousands, if not millions, of job seekers diligently posted their résumés on scores of sites. Then they sat back and waited . . . and waited . . . and waited. You get the idea. Big job sites have their place, of course, but relying solely on an Internet job search is about as effective throwing your résumé into a black hole.

Begin your networking efforts by making a list of people to talk to: teachers, classmates (and their parents), anyone you've worked with, neighbors, members of your church, synogogue, temple or mosque, and anyone you've interned or volunteered with. You can also expand your networking opportunities through the student sections of industry associations; attending or volunteering at industry events, association conferences, career fairs; and through job-shadowing. Keep in mind that only rarely will any of the people on your list be in a position to offer you a job. But whether they know it or not, they probably know someone who knows someone who is. That's why your networking goal is not to ask for a job but the name of someone to talk with. Even when you network with an employer, it's wise to say something like, "You may not have any positions available, but would you know someone I could talk with to find out more about what it's like to work in this field?"

Also, keep in mind that networking is a two-way street. For instance, you may be talking with someone who has a job opening that isn't appropriate for you. If you can refer someone else to the employer, either person may well be disposed to help you someday in the future.

Dial-Up Help

Call your contacts directly, rather than e-mail them. (E-mails are too easy for busy people to ignore, even if they don't mean to.) Explain that you're a recent graduate; that Mr. Jones referred you; and that you're wondering if you could stop by for 10 or 15 minutes at your contact's convenience to find out a little more about how the industry works. If you leave this message as a voicemail, note that you'll call back in a few days to follow up. If you reach your contact directly, expect that they'll say they're too busy at the moment to see you. Ask, "Would you mind if I check back in a couple of weeks?" Then jot down a note in your date book or set up a reminder in your computer calendar and call back when it's time. (Repeat this above scenario as needed, until you get a meeting.)

Once you have arranged to talk with someone in person, prep yourself. Scour industry publications for insightful articles; having up-to-date knowledge about industry trends shows your networking contacts that you're dedicated and focused. Then pull together questions about specific employers and suggestions that will set you apart from the job-hunting pack in your field. The more specific your questions (for instance, about one type of certification versus another), the more likely your contact will see you as an "insider," worthy of passing along to a potential employer. At the end of any networking meeting, ask for the name of someone else who might be able to help you further target your search.

Get a Lift

When you meet with a contact in person (as well as when you run into someone fleetingly), you need an "elevator speech." This is a summary of up to two minutes that introduces who you are, as well as your experience and goals. An elevator speech should be short enough to be delivered during an elevator ride with a potential employer from the ground level to a high floor. In it, it's helpful to show that 1) you know the business involved; 2) you know the company; 3) you're qualified (give your work and educational information); and 4) you're goal-oriented, dependable, and hardworking. You'll be surprised how much information you can include in two minutes. Practice this speech in front of a mirror until you have the key points down very well. It should sound natural though, and you should come across as friendly, confident, and assertive. Remember, good eye contact needs to be part of your presentation as well as your everyday approach when meeting prospective employers or leads.

Get Your Résumé Ready

In addition to your elevator speech, another essential job-hunting tool is your résumé. Basically, a résumé is a little snapshot of you in words, reduced to one 8½ x 11-inch sheet of paper (or, at most, two sheets). You need a résumé whether you're in high school, college, or the workforce, and whether you've never held a job or have had many.

At the top of your résumé should be your heading. This is your name, address, phone numbers, and your e-mail address, which can be a sticking point. E-mail addresses such as sillygirl@yahoo.com or drinkingbuddy@hotmail.com won't score you any points. In fact they're a turn-off. So if you dreamed up your address after a night on the town, maybe it's time to upgrade. (And while we're on the subject, these days, potential employers often check Myspace pages, personal blogs, and Web sites. What's posted there has been known to cost candidates job offers.)

The first section of your résumé is a concise Job Objective: "Entry-level agribusiness sales representative seeking a position with a leading dairy cooperative." These days, with word-processing software, it's easy and smart to adapt your job objective to the position for which you're applying. An alternative way to start a résumé, which some recruiters prefer, is to rework the Job Objective into a Professional Summary. A Professional Summary doesn't mention the position you're seeking, but instead focuses on your job strengths: e.g., "Entry-level agribusiness sales rep; strengths include background in feed, fertilizer, and related markets and ability to contribute as a member of a sales team." Which is better? It's your call.

The body of a résumé typically starts with your Job Experience. This is a chronological list of the positions you've held (particularly the ones that will help you land the job you want). Remember: Never, never fudge anything. It is okay, however, to include volunteer positions and internships on the chronological list, as long as they're noted for what they are.

Next comes your Education section. Note: It's acceptable to flip the order of your Education and Job Experience sections if you're still in high school or don't have significant work experience. Summarize any courses you've taken in the job area you're targeting, any certifications you've achieved, relevant computer knowledge, special seminars, or other school-related experience that will distinguish you. Include your grade average if it's more than 3.0. Don't worry if you haven't finished your degree. Simply write that you're currently enrolled in your program (if you are).

In addition to these elements, other sections may include professional organizations you belong to and any work-related achievements, awards, or recognition you've received. Also, you can have a section for your interests, such as playing piano or soccer (and include any notable achievements regarding your interests, for instance, placed third in Midwest Regional Piano Competition). You should also note other special abilities, such as "Fluent in French," or "Designed own Web site." These sorts of activities will reflect well on you whether or not they are job-related.

You can either include your references or simply note, "References Upon Request." Be sure to ask your references permission to use their name, and alert them to the fact that they may be contacted, before you include them on your résumé. For more information on résumé writing, check out Web sites such as http://www.resume .monster.com.

Craft Your Cover Letter

When you apply for a job either online or by mail, it's appropriate to include a cover letter. A cover letter lets you convey extra information about yourself than doesn't fit or isn't always appropriate in your résumé. For instance, in a cover letter, you can and should mention the name of anyone who referred you to the job. You can go into some detail about the reason you're a great match, given the job description. You can also address any questions that might be raised in the potential employer's mind (for instance, a gap in your résumé). Don't, however, ramble on. Your cover letter should stay focused on your goal: To offer a strong, positive impression of yourself and persuade the hiring manager that you're worth an interview. Your cover letter gives you a chance to stand out from the other applicants and sell yourself. In fact, 23 percent of hiring managers say a candidate's ability to relate his or her experience to the job at hand is a top hiring consideration, according to a Careerbuilder.com survey.

You can write a positive, yet concise cover letter in three paragraphs: An introduction containing the specifics of the job you're applying for; a summary of why you're a good fit for the position and what you can do for the company; and a closing with a request for an interview, your contact information, and thanks. Remember to vary the structure and tone of your cover letter. For instance, don't begin every sentence with "I."

Ace Your Interview

Preparation is the key to acing any job interview. This starts with researching the company or organization you're interviewing with. Start with the firm, group, or agency's own Web site. Explore it thoroughly, read about their products and services, their history, and sales and marketing information. Check out their news releases, links that they provide, and read up on, or Google, members of the management team to get an idea of what they may be looking for in their employees.

Sites such as http://www.hoovers.com enable you to research companies across many industries. Trade publications in any industry (such as *Food Industry News*, *Hotel Business*, and *Hospitality Technology*) are also available at online or in hard copy at many college or public libraries. Don't forget to make a phone call to contacts you have in the organization to get a better idea of the company culture.

Preparation goes beyond research, however. It includes practicing answers to common interview questions:

- *Tell me about yourself.* Don't talk about your favorite bands or your personal history; give a brief summary of your background and interest in the particular job area.
- *Why do you want to work here?* Here's where your research into the company comes into play; talk about the firm's strengths and products or services.

✴ *Why should we hire you?* Now is your chance to sell yourself as a dependable, trustworthy, effective employee.

✴ *Why did you leave your last job?* Keep your answer short; never bad-mouth a previous employer. You can always say something simple, such as, "It wasn't a good fit, and I was ready for other opportunities."

Rehearse your answers, but don't try to memorize them. Responses that are natural and spontaneous come across better. Trying to memorize exactly what you want to say is likely to both trip you up and make you sound robotic.

As for the actual interview, to break the ice, offer a few pleasant remarks about the day, a photo in the interviewer's office, or something else similar. Then, once the interview gets going, listen closely and answer the questions you're asked, versus making any other point that you want to convey. If you're unsure whether your answer was adequate, simply ask, "Did that answer the question?" Show respect, good energy, and enthusiasm, and be upbeat. Employers are looking for workers who are enjoyable to be around, as well as good workers. Show that you have a positive attitude and can get along well with others by not bragging during the interview, overstating your experience, or giving the appearance of being too self-absorbed. Avoid one-word answers, but at the same time don't blather. If you're faced with a silence after giving your response, pause for a few seconds, and then ask, "Is there anything else you'd like me to add?" Never look at your watch and turn your cell phone off before an interview.

Near the interview's end, the interviewer is likely to ask you if you have any questions. Make sure that you have a few prepared, for instance:

✴ *"Tell me about the production process."*

✴ *"What's your biggest short-term challenge?"*

✴ *"How have recent business trends affected the company?"*

✴ *"Is there anything else that I can provide you with to help you make your decision?"*

✴ *"When will you make your hiring decision?"*

During a first interview, never ask questions like, "What's the pay?" "What are the benefits?" or "How much vacation time will I get?"

Find the *Right Look*

Appropriate dress and grooming is also essential to interviewing success. For business jobs and many other occupations, it's appropriate to come to an interview in a nice (not stuffy) suit. However, different fields have various dress codes. In the music business, for instance, "business casual" reigns for many jobs. This is a slightly modified look, where slacks and a jacket are just fine for a man, and a nice skirt and blouse and jacket or sweater are acceptable for a woman. Dressing overly "cool" will usually backfire.

In general, tend to all the basics from shoes (no sneakers, sandals, or overly high heels) to outfits (no short skirts for women). Women should also avoid attention-getting necklines. Keep jewelry to a minimum. Tattoos and body jewelry are becoming more acceptable, but if you can take out piercings (other than a simple stud in your ear), you're better off. Similarly, unusual hairstyles or colors may bias an employer against you, rightly or wrongly. Make sure your hair is neat and acceptable (consider getting a haircut). Also go light on the makeup, self-tanning products, body scents, and other grooming agents. Don't wear a baseball cap or any other type of hat, and by all means, take off your sunglasses!

Beyond your physical appearance, you already know to be well bathed to minimize odor (leave your home early if you tend to sweat, so you can cool off in private), use a breath mint (especially if you smoke) make good eye contact, smile, speak clearly using proper English (or Spanish), use good posture (don't slouch), offer a firm handshake, and arrive within five minutes of your interview. (If you're unsure of where you're going, Mapquest or Google Map it and consider making a dry run to the site so you won't be late.) First impressions can make or break your interview.

Remember to *Follow Up*

After your interview, send a thank-you note. This thoughtful gesture will separate you from most of the other candidates. It demonstrates your ability to follow through, and it catches your prospective employer's attention one more time. In a 2005 Careerbuilder.com survey, nearly 15 percent of 650 hiring managers said they wouldn't hire someone who failed to send a thank-you letter after the interview. Thirty-two percent say they would still consider the candidate, but would think less of him or her.

So do you hand write or e-mail the thank you letter? The fact is that format preferences vary. One in four hiring managers prefer to receive a thank-you note in e-mail form only; 19 percent want the e-mail, followed up with a hard copy; 21 percent want a typed hard-copy only, and 23 percent prefer just a handwritten note. (Try to check with an assistant on the format your potential employer prefers). Otherwise, sending an e-mail and a handwritten copy is a safe way to proceed.

Winning an Offer

There are no sweeter words to a job hunter than, "We'd like to hire you." So naturally, when you hear them, you may be tempted to jump at the offer. *Don't.* Once an employer wants you, he or she will usually give you some time to make your decision and get any questions you may have answered. Now is the time to get specific about salary, benefits, and negotiate some of these points. If you haven't already done so, check out salary ranges for your position and area of the country on sites such as Payscale.com, Salary.com, and Salaryexpert.com (basic info is free; specific requests are not). Also find out what sort of benefits similar jobs offer. Then don't be afraid to negotiate in a diplomatic way. Asking for better terms is reasonable and expected. You may worry that asking the employer to bump up his or her offer may jeopardize your job, but handled intelligently, negotiating for yourself may in fact be a way to impress your future employer and get a better deal for yourself.

After you've done all the hard work that successful job-hunting requires, you may be tempted to put your initiative into autodrive. However, the efforts you made to land your job—from clear communication to enthusiasm-are necessary now to pave your way to continued success. As Danielle Little, a human-resources assistant, says, "You must be enthusiastic and take the initiative. There is an urgency to prove yourself and show that you are capable of performing any and all related tasks. If your manager notices that you have potential, you will be given additional responsibilities, which will help advance your career." So do your best work on the job, and build your credibility. Your payoff will be career advancement and increased earnings.

Index